THE NIGHT
IS GONE

THE NIGHT IS GONE

WHY POPE FRANCIS CANONIZES CARDINAL NEWMAN

Gerald Jumbam Nyuykongmo

The Night Is Gone

Copyright © 2019 by Gerald Jumbam Nyuykongmo. All rights reserved.

No part of this publication may be reproduced, stored in a retrieval system or transmitted in any way by any means, electronic, mechanical, photocopy, recording or otherwise without the prior permission of the author except as provided by USA copyright law.

The opinions expressed by the author are not necessarily those of URLink Print and Media.

1603 Capitol Ave., Suite 310 Cheyenne, Wyoming USA 82001
1-888-980-6523 | admin@urlinkpublishing.com

URLink Print and Media is committed to excellence in the publishing industry.

Book design copyright © 2019 by URLink Print and Media. All rights reserved.

Published in the United States of America

ISBN 978-1-64367-802-3 (Paperback)
ISBN 978-1-64367-801-6 (Digital)

29.08.19

To Sr. BIANCO Maria Grazia:

one of the finest contemporary scholars I have come across,
in the example of Newmanian faith, friendship and philosophy.

NEWMAN'S PRAYER TO ALL CHRISTIANS

O Lion of the Tribe of Judah, the root of David, …give grace to every one in his own place to fight Thy battle well. Be with Thy missionaries in pagan lands, put right words into their mouths, prosper their labours, and sustain them under their sufferings with Thy consolations, and carry them on, even through torment and blood (if it be necessary), to their reward in heaven. Give the grace of wisdom to those in high station, that they may neither yield to fear, nor be seduced by flattery. Make them prudent as serpents, and simple as doves. Give Thy blessing to all preachers and teachers, that they may speak Thy words and persuade their hearers to love Thee. Be with all faithful servants of Thine, whether in low station or in high, who mix in the world; instruct them how to speak and how to act every hour of the day, so as to preserve their own souls from evil and to do good to their companions and associates. Teach us, one and all, to live in thy presence and to see Thee, our Great Leader and Thy Cross—and thus to fight valiantly and to overcome, that at the last we may sit down with Thee in Thy Throne, as Thou also hast overcome and art set down with Thy Father in His Throne.

ACKNOWLEDGEMENTS

I am very grateful to Sr. Bianco Maria Grazia and Fr Raffaele Pettenuzzo for their spiritual guidance, care and encouragements during these years. I thank the Director of ISSR Mater Ecclesiae (Angelicum) Fr. SALVATI Giuseppe Marco, for his leadership and the whole university family for providing me a calm academic environment.

I am so grateful to Fr Hermann Geissler (who has given the book a beautiful Foreword), Fr Philip, Sr. Maria Birgit and to the whole *The Work* congregation in Rome for their motivation and inspirations. The Newman Association of America has during these years motivated me to write on subjects they proposed for their annual meetings. I am grateful to all of these wonderful people and institutions. I thank friends and brothers like Fr. Ger Fitzgerald, Fr. Eric and Fr. Lorenzo Varrecchia, and Mr. Emmanuel Kongyuy Jumbam.

Chinua Achebe's non-fictional works have guided me especially in the light of the idea of African theology - I am grateful to his insights.

THE AUTHOR'S PREFACE

These pages are the fruit of contemplations when I was going through (in my own humble way) some trying moments similar to some upsetting circumstances of Newman's life. The thoughts came to me in packages, and the life of this saint lightened my heart, as it panted for peace.. Because his way of life, to some of his contemporaries was messy and untidy, his ways have influence men and women of today especially those who live untidy burdensome lives. I count it a privilege to have had *The Night is Gone* prepared for the public at this hour, the year of the canonization of my saint John Henry Newman; nor can I refrain from hoping that many who do not know this holy man would see in him, through this work, the emblematic beauty of the Church's unwearied global love. Great genius such as Newman's cannot be reduced to simple one-line elucidations. People like him who become legendary even in their life time, remain more than ever legendary, and more than ever spoken about. What sets Newman out from the ordinary is that at some very deep level he practiced and penned what his countryman and poet, William Wordsworth called,

> "the very world, which is the world
> Of all of us – the place where in the end,
> We find our happiness, or not at all."

The world is all the brighter for the lighting of a mighty light. His canonization is an event of our age, over which the most staunch Protestant or Pagan can celebrate as sincerely as any member of the Catholic community. I have today, the unspeakable satisfaction of sending *The Night is Gone* to the world, a book whose writing has given me huge joy and whose conclusion has received great enjoyment in my heart, enjoyment that has been attended by so much anxiety and not a little peril. Three years, you will see, have left the traces of "wear and tear" on me, after the publishing of my first book on Newman, but produced no change in the high esteem and profound veneration, with which I have in my saint Newman. I am thus bound to him by the strong ties of personal gratitude - profoundly indebted to him in the recent breakthroughs I have made in intellectual and spiritual life.

"The greatest theologian of the century, the sweetest singer of the world unseen, the gentlest and the noblest of Englishmen"[1] is saint. The steadfast faith that has marked him out as a prophet to a disbelieving generation, the wide and tender kindnesses that in Newman transfigured zeal to the excellence of a fan of Christian friendship, the name of Newman brings with it memories, and raises a host of affectionate feelings in me. Consequently, this book has seen the light of day thanks to personal reasons, but particularly to communicate at the request of today's faith exigencies, the principles of a man who took time to think, took time to write, took time to believe: John Henry Newman. In so far as this book is a spiritual testament of a very intellectual character, it aims to break new ground in several ways: in highlighting the relevance of Newman to contemporary faith; in shedding fresh light on Newman's educational charisma, in evincing the fecundity of one of the greatest theologians of our times; and in drawing attention to Newman's contribution to the spirit of new evangelization sweeping the entire Church today.

By a very rare gift he knows how to kindle hope in hearts that are failing, and with caring yet piercing irony smiles away the biases and bigotries of taxing contemporaries. He is a saint who tells you to keep going even when you are confused and abandoned by unexpected quarters. I am wholly aware that it is the deep affection and high esteem in which he is held in me that has produced these pages.

As all the noise and dust of disagreement around his name has subsided with the waning years, the soul of NEWMAN, is now (in his own words) shining "like a star, exalting the minds which turn towards it; and that when his precepts have been forgotten in the generations, he will still teach mankind by the lofty eloquence of

---

[1] Newman Reader, "Birmingham Daily Gazette", in *The Press on Cardinal Newman*, 36.

his example." His life is one great effort for the regeneration of the human race; that is what we celebrate in *The Night is Gone*, that is what *The Night is Gone* celebrate in this saint.

I am conscious of the fact that to wed Pope Francis with Cardinal Newman – a thing I openly do here – is a stroke of courage. To try to show that Francis' theology has something to do with Newman's, is to push courage still further. The clouds of controversy, in which Francis is most concerned, are still alive. Yet my attentive and all-pervading study of Newman, Vatican II and post Vatican II has unlocked my mind to many motivating things about this holy man regarding current Christianity. One of such discoveries is that though he hardly calls the name Newman, Pope Francis' pontificate is that which has had the closest empathy to John Henry Newman's sensibilities. What Francis is doing today to the streets of the world is what Newman's idol patron Philip Neri did to the streets of Rome. Newman esteemed and acclaimed the simple Philip Neri. It hasn't surprised me that providence has appointed Pope Francis to canonize Cardinal Newman. They who breathe the same intellectual air (Newman was considered by some detractors as a Jesuit) as Newman, they who go through the misunderstandings and suffer similar calumnies he suffered, they who believe with him that "truth can fight its own battle," such must be the best, if not the only true recorders of his life. That is why Pope Francis stands in the most satisfactory, the most favorable and the most beneficial position to canonize this great saint and scholar of all times.

FOREWORD

By FR. HERMANN GEISSLER, FSO

Director of the International Centre of Newman Friends

Rome

On October 13th, 2019, Pope Francis will canonize Blessed John Henry Newman (1801-1890). There is no doubt that Newman belongs to the most significant thinkers of the modern age. In his Christmas address to the Roman Curia in 2010, Benedict XVI spoke of the great English Cardinal – whom he had beatified earlier that year on September 19th – and emphasized Newman's prophetic significance for our own day, stating that we all "must learn from Newman's three conversions, because they were steps along a spiritual path." He then mentioned the decisive role of the conscience: "The path of Newman's conversions is a path of conscience – not a path of self-asserting subjectivity but, on the contrary, a path of obedience to the truth that was gradually opening to him."

Newman's first conversion was his conversion to faith in the living God. Until that moment, Newman thought like the average people of his time and like the average people of today, who do not simply exclude the existence of God, but consider it as something uncertain, something with no essential role to play in their lives. In his conversion, Newman recognized that God and the soul, man's spiritual identity, constitute what really counts. This conversion was a Copernican revolution. What had previously seemed unreal and secondary became now decisive and essential. Newman continually revisits the need to "realize" faith in God, to enter into his truth, to orient oneself to God so that God might influence one's practical life. After all, for Newman the risk is that human beings abandon God and live their lives without God. Newman foresees this apostasy.

Today, he might exhort us to turn ourselves to what counts, to be aware of God's presence, to be witnesses even in the face of those who waver, those who are distant, and the many of our day who seek the truth.

Newman discovered the truth of God in the depths of his conscience. His journey of life shows us how he followed the tender voice of conscience – as if by a "kindly light" – and how he opened himself to the truth and obeyed its commands. Above all, Newman is a master and witness of the conscience in its authentic meaning, something necessary to rediscover today. For Newman, conscience is not something purely subjective, but the echo of God's voice in our hearts. Obedience to his conscience rendered him interiorly free from human ties to a career, honour, and a profession; it left him free for God, for the truth and for the Church of Christ. With his own life, Newman shows us that conscience is the advocate of truth in our hearts. "Conscience is the most secret core and sanctuary of a man. There he is alone with God, whose voice echoes in his depths" (Vatican II, *Gaudium et spes,* 16). We, too, should have the courage to give ear to this voice even if it sets us apart from others, for we feel obligated to move towards its indications and are able to live as free and authentic people.

Obedience to the truth led Newman into the harbour of the Catholic Church. It is true that Newman's life is, in its very essence, a life in obedience to his conscience. After his first conversion, he became aware of the great truths of Christianity. He led the Oxford Movement, striving to reform the Church of England according to the model of the early Church and trying to preserve it from the harmful influence of liberalism in religion. Thus, he came ever closer to the Catholic Church and finally, after much searching, he arrived at the conviction of the necessity of his conversion. One might say that Newman's inner journey is a defence of the Church in the form of a witness. As Paul VI says, "Modern man listens more willingly to witnesses than to teachers" (*Evangelii nuntiandi,* 41), and so in our time a life such as Newman's has a greater effect than many theoretical arguments. Perhaps we could say that a real apology for the Church in our days must have the form of testimony in order to be credible and convincing to others. Today, more than ever, the Church needs similar testimonies that present a coherence between life and thought.

Real faith in God, genuine obedience to the voice of conscience, and credible witness to the Church: these are only some elements that characterize Newman's life and make him an eminently important figure for our times. This book, "*THE NIGHT IS GONE. Why Pope Francis Canonizes Cardinal Newman*", shows us how these and other reasons urge Pope Francis to present Newman as a Saint to the whole Church. I sincerely congratulate Fr. Gerald Jumbam Nyuykongmo for the profound contributions published in this book, hoping that it finds many readers who are led to a personal relationship to Newman and, through him, to a deeper faith in God a more profound love for His Church.

Chapter One

THE BEATING HEART IS MERCY

The decision to take "Out of Shadows and Images into the Truth" as the epitaph on his tombstone, was the most fitting homage John Henry Newman paid his entire life. This maxim - Ex umbris et imaginibus in veritatem – is more than an epitaph: it is the defining principle that ruled Newman, from the beginning to the end. The most brilliant expression of the virtue of truth in Newman, is dramatized in the *Apologia Pro Vita Sua*. There, he sets out to defend himself against a "scurrilous public attack by Charles Kingsley" on the sincerity of his actions and on the truth about his newfound home, the Roman Catholic Church. Newman expresses his disgust at the way Kingsley focuses on him, and "certainly, here was an opportunity to practice what Newman had so often preached, that one must suffer for the truth."[2]

However, like Paul, in the Acts of the Apostles, Newman's search for the truth had thrown him from his high intellectual horse into a spiritual turmoil. In the Acts of the Apostles, Paul reflects on this remarkable experience:

> "Thus I journeyed to Damascus…At midday…I saw on the way a light from heaven, brighter than the sun, shining round me and those who journeyed with me. And when we had all fallen to the ground, I heard a voice saying to me in the Hebrew language, 'Saul, Saul, why do you persecute me?'" (Acts 26:12-14)

---

[2] I. KER, *John Henry Newman*, Oxford University Press, 381.

Newman's spiritual turmoil would eventually direct him to seek out assistance, not merely in intellectual curiosity or scholarly debates, but also in the power of God's mercy. From the high horse of rabbinical scholarship Paul would bow down before Ananias; and from the high horse of Oxford scholarship, Newman would bow down before Fr Dominic Barberi. Their conversion stories demonstrate a certain interconnection between the search for truth and the power of mercy in human life.

I should like to say that this is not just another essay on Newman's search for the truth, but an essay about how truth and mercy wedded in the rich spiritual journey of J. H. Newman and how these things are relevant to us today. Let us now plunge into the deeper meanings of truth and mercy in the life of Cardinal Newman. We begin with the truth.

The 'fake news' analysis of media houses today seems to be getting exaggerated. But there is something certainly true in this analysis. Someone has called the present times the post-truth generation. In fact, the media is a powerful metaphor of how this postmodern era more often than not, turns truth into a social construct, creates their own 'truths' and allows ethical issues shift with the shifting political polls. Indeed we are living in a generation where dishonesty has become commonplace, and truth more often than not, is sacrificed in the altar of political or religious correctness. Speaking about speaking the truth in today's media houses, the famous American film star and producer Denzel Washington made some statements; he said, "one of the effects of too much information is the need to be first, not even to be true anymore."

"In our society, now it's just first — who cares, get it out there. We don't care who it hurts. We don't care who we destroy. We don't care if it's true,"

What is striking about Denzel Washington here is his love of truth. People are losing confidence not only in media houses but in cultural, political, and religious structures, that no more represent what life truly is.

Because John Henry Newman allowed himself to be led by the kindly light of Truth, he built on Augustine of Hippo's example, and was among the thinkers of his day that searched for truth in all the hidden corners of the world. On the preeminence of truth, Newman inscribes the following epigrammatic words in a letter to an Anglican friend:

> Truth can fight its battle. It has a reality in it, which shivers to pieces swords of earth. As far as we are not on the side of truth, *we* shall shiver to bits, and I am willing it should be so.[3]

The complexity of the world we live in, has made it a difficult feat to find truth. Newman believed that passion, patience, doubt, certitude and grace were hallmarks of the search for the truth. Such virtues would lead Newman to philosophically reexamine his life and the world he lives in:

> I look out of myself into the world of men, and there I see a sight which fills me with unspeakable distress. The world seems simply to give the lie to that great truth, of which my whole being is so full; and the effect upon me is, in consequence, as a matter of necessity, as confusing as if it denied that I am in existence myself.[4]

On this, Newman would argue that since he looks into the mirror and sees that he is, he has no difficulty in looking into this busy concrete world and seeing the reflection of God who created the world.

Newman believed in the Church and believed that she was the bulwark and dispenser of Truth. He didn't like, seeing truth and the Church being caricatured by people who knew little about it. He would not fear to tackle high profiled personalities like Gladstone when they engaged in such aberrations. An example in his writings

---

[3] J. H. NEWMAN, *The Letters and Diaries of J. H. Newman* To R. Belaney, 25.01.1841.

[4] J. H. Newman, *Apologia Pro Vita Sua,* Penguin Books,London 1994, 216.

of what we are talking about is *The Letter to the Duke of Norfolk*. Important here is to consider what prompted the writing of the letter. The letter came in the aftermath of the First Vatican Council's definition of the doctrine of papal infallibility. Gladstone the English Prime minister had infuriated Newman with his statement that Catholics could not be trusted citizens of the country because one could not simultaneously be faithful to the Catholic Church and loyal to the State. Newman believed this to be a misrepresentation of English Catholicism. For him, the affirmation of Gladstone was the night of falsehood to be countered with the light of truth; and Newman skillfully corrects this fabrication in his *Letter to the Duke of Norfolk*. After having maintained that Catholics are duty bound to obey the Pope in his divine function, Newman reminds his countrymen in this letter that it is not wholly Catholic theology that says a thing is good or bad merely because an authority says so, as he concludes thus: "Certainly, if I am obliged to bring religion into after-dinner toasts (which indeed does not seem quite the thing), I shall drink – to the Pope, if you please, - still, to Conscience first, and to the pope afterwards".[5] The event of this letter to the Duke paints the picture of Newman's investigative excellence and intellectual honesty in the quest for religious truth. Ultimately, it confirmed the profundity of Newman's comprehension of the Catholic Church.

Another masterpiece of Newman written in defense of the truth is *Lectures on the Present Position of Catholics in England*. In this particular book, he posited that the fiercest enemy of truth was prejudice. By prejudice here he meant pre-judgment, judgment by anticipation.[6] Defamation, falsification and parody of the Catholic faith had become a natural phenomenon in Newman's England. No matter how much you were gifted, no matter how much you contributed to nation building, to be a Catholic was to be a profligate. In fact, in this England, the Anglicans (in the words of Newman himself) were "kinder even to their dogs and cats than us"[7]. So much dirt was

---

[5] J. H. NEWMAN, *A Letter to the Duke of Norfolk*.
[6] J. H. NEWMAN, *Lectures on the Present Position of Catholics in England*, London 1908, 227.
[7] J. H. NEWMAN, *Lectures on the Present Position of Catholics in England*, 264.

flung on Catholicism. To be able to strip the Catholic church of these fallacies and fiction, Newman exposed prejudice for what it truly was. Prejudice, he said, "can tell falsehoods to our dishonor by the score"; it is "jealous of truth"; **prejudiced** people "if they condescend to listen for a moment to your arguments it is in order to pick holes in them.."[8] In the context of Newman's England, prejudice tamed facts, misstated Church doctrines, diffused wild allegation, defamed the character of holy men. Newman, faithful to his principle of defender of truth, became one of the greatest warriors against prejudice during his times. He did this so entirely and valiantly especially in his *Lectures on the Present Position of Catholics in England*. As a consequence, the following homage by *Catholic Times* was paid him immediately news came out that he was dead:

> John Henry Newman conquered prejudice and won universal affection by the noble simplicity of his character, his fearless and unswerving adhesion to truth, his high and lofty ideal of duty, and his incomparable intellectual gifts. Those who are old enough to remember the outbursts of anti-Catholic feeling which in years gone by were so frequent amongst the Protestants of Great Britain cease not to wonder at the change which has come over the land. How much of this change is due to the part played by Cardinal NEWMAN in the national life! (…) And as he found light himself he diffused it (…) and the Catholic body gradually obtained a fuller toleration.[9]

Newman's only longing was to be truth's devotee: "My desire hath been to have Truth for my chiefest friend, and no enemy but error".[10]

---

[8] J. H. NEWMAN, *Lectures on the Present Position of Catholics in England*, 314.
[9] J. Glancey(ed.), "Catholic Times", in *The Press on Cardinal Newman With A Short Sketch Of His Life*, (undated), in http://www.newmanreader.org/biography/death/index.html, 51-52.
[10] J. H. NEWMAN, The Via Media of the Anglican Church, Vol I, Westminster 1978,XII.

In fact, in the words of Paul Shrimpton, Newman " (…) speaks to us with moral and spiritual urgency, determined that neither habit, familiarity, nor prejudice will prevent us from being open to the truth, including the truth about ourselves".[11]

Newman had a very deep sense of personal freedom and fully believed in what he called an innermost "intercourse between myself and my Maker." To him, influence and personal example were essential qualities for the quest for truth. He preferred those whose personal example influenced the life of other men and women to dedicate their lives to truth:

> [Truth] has been upheld in the world not as a system, not by books, not by argument, nor by temporal power, but by the personal influence of… men… who are at once the teachers and the patterns of it.[12]

When truth is incarnated in persons, it is no more in need of sermons from pulpits or podiums. That is the message of Newman.

Among the elements that show how Newman witnessed to the truth, the event of the writing of the *Apologia Pro Vita Sua* was the most outstanding. Just about enjoying his membership into the Catholic Church he got the shock of his life when news of Kingsley's outrageous attack came to him something like this: "O the chicanery, the wholesale fraud, the vile hypocrisy, the conscience-killing tyranny of Rome! We have not far to seek for an evidence of it. There's Father Newman to wit: one living specimen is worth a hundred dead ones. He, a Priest writing of Priests, tells us that lying is never any harm."[13] Newman refused to accept the calumny of Kingsley and in his own words: "I do not like to be called to my face a liar and a knave; nor should I be doing my duty to my faith or to my name, if I were to suffer it. I know I have done nothing to deserve such an insult. And if I prove this, as I hope to do, I must not care for such incidental

---

[11] P. SHRIMPTON, *The 'Making of Men'*, Gracewing, Leominster 2014, xliii.
[12] Newman, *Fifteen Sermons*, 96-97.
[13] See I. KER, *John Henry Newman*, Oxford University Press, 536.

annoyances as are involved in the process."[14] With these words he went on a long, painful and fruitful journey to defending himself against untruth. He did it excellently in his *Apologia Pro Vita Sua*.

However, during this defense of self, Newman discovers that "there is something deeper in our differences than the accident of external circumstances; and that we need the interposition of a Power, greater than human teaching and human argument, to make our beliefs true and our minds one".[15] That thing for Newman, would be God's loving mercy on man. If ever there was a date-making event in Newman's life this was it; it would be what I call the primacy of mercy in the narrative of his rich spiritual life and in the story of all holy men and women. Pope Francis brings this into the arena, in his ministry; and in his own words: "Once mercy has been truly experienced, it is impossible to turn back. It grows constantly and changes our lives. It is an authentic new creation: it brings about a new heart, capable of loving to the full, and it purifies our eyes to perceive our needs."[16] Aptly, Newman affirms: "all the logic in the world would not have made me move faster towards Rome than I did"[17]. God's mercy and the motherly welcoming of the Church brought him to the Catholic Church. In fact, Newman knew very well that in the act of conversion God takes the upper hand, and then man cooperates as we read in John's Gospel, "You did not choose me, but I chose you and appointed you so that you might go and bear fruit—fruit that will last." (John 15: 16). That to me is how truth and mercy interplay in the rich spiritual life of John Henry Newman. It is that power of God's mercy I will explore now.

Of all the decisions that have revolutionized the Catholic Church in this century, few have been more compelling than the courageous decision of Pope John XXIII to open a Second Vatican Council. In a speech that began that Ecumenical Council, John XXIII spelt out what the Council meant in our times in the following words:

---

[14] J. H. Newman, *Apologia Pro Vita Sua*, Penguin Books, London 2004, 17.
[15] J. H. Newman, *Apologia Pro Vita Sua*, Penguin Books, London 2004, 158-159.
[16] POPE FRANCIS, Apostolic Letter, *Misericordia Et Misera*, 16.
[17]

> The Church has always opposed ... errors, and often condemned them with the utmost severity. Today, however, Christ's Bride (the Church) prefers the balm of mercy to the arm of severity. She believes that, present needs are best served by explaining more fully the purport of her doctrines, rather than by publishing condemnations.[18]

The effects of these words were far-reaching not only to the Ecumenical Council Fathers but its message on the 'the balm of mercy' has been all-embracing in the Church after the Council. So remarkable and extensive have been the benefits of the message, that since the days of Pope John XXIII to our own, the Church has found mercy as an original way of bringing a breath of fresh air back into the world. The mercy of God, Pope Francis says, is "the beating heart of the Gospel".[19] This is in keeping with the Gospel message: "I desire mercy, not sacrifice," (Matthew 9:13). This second part of the presentation is about the power of God's mercy in John Henry Newman. This second half of my presentation is, for many reasons, of the highest importance.

The most exciting element which graphically pictures the work of mercy in Newman's life was the event of his conversion to the Catholic Church. To be able to fathom the profundity of God's mercy shown Newman in his conversion story, it is important to understand the amount of hate speech Newman spewed on Catholicism during his Anglican days. He grew up believing that the Roman Catholic Church was a symbol of the Antichrist foretold in the Bible. His abhorrence - as an Anglican - of the Catholic Church was razor-sharp. A man who hurled curses and invective at the Catholic Church like 'crafty', 'obstinate', 'malicious', 'cruel', 'unnatural', 'demoniac', could not but be grateful to this very Church for inestimable mercy shown

---

[18] JOHN XXIII, "Pope John XXIII's Opening Address of Vatican Council II", in *Marians of the Immaculate Conception*, http://www.marian.org/news/Pope-John-XXIIIs-Opening-Address-of-Vatican-Council-II-5666, October 11, 1962.

[19] POPE FRANCIS, *Misericordia Et Misera*, 12.

a detractor like him. Come to think of it, in 1844, just some months before his conversion to Rome, Newman was still at daggers with the Roman Catholic Church: "I have no existing sympathies with Roman Catholics. I hardly even, even abroad, was at one of their services – I know none of them. I do not like what I hear of them".[20] The mercies of God began visiting his soul. This period immediately before his conversion, he calls his Anglican 'death-bed': "A death-bed has scarcely a history; it is a tedious decline, with seasons of rallying, and seasons of falling back."[21] This 'death-bed' symbolizes the vision of God's mercy in Newman's life. On the 9th of October 1845, he was received into the Catholic Church. He will see his conversion into Catholicism as a manifestation of God's mercy in his life:

> I have had more to try and afflict me in various ways as a Catholic than as an Anglican; but never for a moment have I wished myself back; never have I ceased to thank my Maker for His Mercy in enabling me to make the great change, and never has He let me feel forsaken by Him, or in distress, or any kind of religious trouble.[22]

God's boundless mercy has visited Newman, forgiven his youth, and brought him closer to Jesus, as he himself would lament in prayer: "O my God, that overpowering love took me captive. Was any boyhood so impious as some years of mine! Did I not in fact dare Thee to do Thy worst? Ah, how I struggled to get free from Thee; but Thou art stronger than I and hast prevailed. I have not a word to say, but to bow down in awe before the depths of Thy love."[23]

This is the profound impact of mercy on those who honestly search for the truth.

---

[20] LD, To Henry Edward Manning, 16 November 1844.
[21] J. H. NEWMAN, *Apologia Pro Vita Sua*, chapter 4.
[22] In his 'Postscript' to *The Letter to the Duke of Norfolk*, Newman would lament in expression of this mercy shown him:
[23] J. H. NEWMAN, *Meditations and Devotions*, Longmans, Green and Co., London 1907, 399 – 400.

Life is a great teacher. Right from childhood days Newman had learned the virtue of pardon from his parents. As a young boy in Trinity College he met the humiliation of his life when he failed his examinations. It brought him untold psychological suffering. He lamented to his father in a letter:

> The pain it gives me to be obliged to inform you and my Mother of it I cannot express. What I feel on my own account is indeed nothing at all, compared with the idea that I have disappointed you.[24]

The forgiving consolation of Newman's parents when he failed examinations would teach him the importance of mercy in life. The mercy of a human father and a human mother, and therefore the mercy of our Heavenly Father, God. Later on as an Anglican Church man, Newman would meet another embarrassing experience in Oxford when his authorities would expose and discredit him as a result of the 90th article on *Tracts for the Times*.

Such humbling events in his life rather than crush him, strengthened his faith in God. They made him understand that to be holy is to be dependent on God as he appeals in prayer: "without You (God) I can do nothing, and You are there where Your Church is and Your Sacraments."[25], "how merciful Thou hast been to me (…) Not for my merit, but from Thy free and bountiful love."[26]

What then can we today, learn from the story of Newman's life? His life can teach the genuine seeker of truth, that however intellectually absorbed he is in digging out truth in his private study, he will do effective work if he is dependent on God, if he is merciful to the faltering, if he dialogues with his detractors, if he is patient with the ignorant, and if he is attentive to the cry of the disadvantaged.

---

[24] J. H, Newman, *LD*, 1:94 JHN to Mr. Newman.
[25] J. H. NEWMAN, *Meditations and Devotions*, Longmans, Green and Co., London 1907,
[26] J. H. NEWMAN, *Meditations and Devotions*, Longmans, Green and Co., London 1907, 398.

Newman's burning passion for truth spread through his entire life. But the epicenter of this engagement is the event of his conversion from Anglicanism to Catholicism. The reciprocity between truth and mercy, between person and community, between conscience and conversion quickly acquired an epic quality in that particular moment of his life. He would look for truth in the privacy of his Oxford study, but would find its plenitude in the merciful welcoming of the Catholic Church.

God's mercy has an indescribable power. Newman enlightens our minds with the light of truth and enkindles our hearts with the power of mercy. Joseph Ratzinger (who later became Pope Benedict XVI) identified this and positioned Newman in contemporary context with the aid of the following succinct words:

> The characteristic of the great Doctor of the Church it seems to me, is, that he teaches not only through his thought and speech but also by his life... If this is so, then Newman belongs to the great teachers of the Church, because he both touches our hearts and enlightens our thinking.[27]

Today, few Christian thinkers have done a winning intellectual battle over the past century, against falsehood and infidelity, than Cardinal John Henry Newman. Perhaps it was an excellent idea for John Allen to confer on him the fitting title of Catholicism's patron saint of relevance.[28] One of the reasons for this relevance would unquestionably be that Newman appears with excellent answers to nearly all hot-button issues of the Church today. One of such is the centrality of truth and mercy in the life of Christians demonstrated by the pages of this essay. This in a nutshell is the relevance of this modern voice, Newman, today.

---

[27] J. RATZINGER, *First centenary of the Death of Cardinal John Henry Newman*, a Presentation of 28 April 1990, http://www.thepapalvisit.org.uk/Cardinal-Newman/The-Popes-on-Newman/Pope-Benedict-XVI-on-Newman.

[28] JOHN ALLEN, "John Henry Newman could become the patron saint of relevance, in *Crux*", January 23, 2016, https://cruxnow.com/church/2016/01/23/john-henry-newman-could-become-the-patron-saint-of-relevance/

We frequently entrap ourselves in the same tricky web as the disciples did on the road to Emmaus, paying attention to what seems to be losing ground, not to where we are destined to go. In those moments, we can so easily mistake thorns for roses, and roses for thorns. Newman's faith journey has much to teach those willing to listen. Therefore, let us accompany Newman in his inspiring journey, in seeking the truth. By combining truth with mercy in the discovery of the life of Newman, I have tried to demonstrate his spiritual accomplishments in the full context of his times, and hence in a fresh light. What emerges from this narrative is the image of a Christian philosopher and a holy man, capable not just of pursuing truth but of trusting in the divine mercies of the Maker of Heaven and Earth. It is not enough to talk about truth, or else we are nothing more than spectators. We must act like Newman, by opening our hearts to God's surprises while we seek out the truth. By so doing, Newman would meet a surprise, a surprise in mercy which would bring him to conversion, to his final destination – the Catholic Church. There are good reasons to conclude that the God-who-is-Truth is the God-who-is-Mercy. No doubt Pope Francis advocates today: "Now is the time to unleash the creativity of mercy."[29] Today, for all those truly dedicated to offering their lives to the pursuit of God, and therefore to the pursuit of the truth, the greatest test that Newman and the Catholic Church can offer, is the test of mercy.

---

[29] POPE FRANCIS, Apostolic Letter, *Misericordia Et Misera*, 18.

Chapter Two

NEWMAN AND NEW EVANGELIZATION

John Henry Newman, once spoke the truth about his entire life in few words: "from first to last, education…has been my line."[30]. To him education is not formation for life, education is existence itself. And "Education is the most powerful weapon", Nelson Mandela had said, "which you can use to change the world."[31] Undoubtedly education is the lifeblood of human society - the crucial component that has given the Church energy and fortified its sanctuaries with many millions for Christ. But theological education would in the main, be Newman's most arresting arsenal, for, he held that university teaching without Theology is simply unphilosophical – that is, unsound, arbitrary, truncated. When, saint John Paul II on the 9th of June 1979, at the sanctuary of Mogila in Nowa Huta, aired the expression "new evangelization" for the first time, little did he know he was a stimulus that would trigger off a remarkable missionary movement. New evangelization - the topmost business of the Church today – is education indeed.

Post-Vatican II Popes have put the issue of new evangelization front and center on the ecclesial stage. Pope Benedict XVI took over from the Polish Pope and created the Pontifical Council for the Promotion of the New Evangelization. Pope Francis' duty call

---

[30] IAN KER, *Newman's Idea of a University and its Relevance for the 21st Century*, (April 2011), 1.
[31] NELSON MANDELA, *Speech at Launch of Mindset Network, Johannesburg*, 16 July 2003.

to countries considered destitute by the world and his voice-of-the-voiceless public position in encyclicals and exhortations, have brought us to the consciousness of this new and revitalizing spirit animating missionary work in our times. These Popes spell out the mission of "new evangelization". as unlike the other kind of missionary work best labeled the Good News. They understand it as pastoral attention heading not merely for the pagan or the heathen, but most especially for the baptized and the Christian.

The African Church today looks at it from the point of view of Small Christian Communities (Church in the neighborhood). In Europe the coat of arms of Cardinal Newman, that compelling catchphrase *Cor ad Cor Loquitur* renders best the spirit of New Evangelization in the West. Heart speaks to heart. God speaks to man heart to heart and then man's heart speaks to his fellowman. And therefore in a cultural context eaten up by the cancer of individualism, relativism and spiritual liberalism, there is a crying need for the Sacred Heart of Jesus to speak to Europe's heart once more.

Cor ad Cor loquitur suggests the Most Holy Trinity. In the Trinity is the language of love and dialogue. Inevitably God wills that men and women should among themselves raise, improve and advance the exchange of feelings between hearts, *cor ad cor,* since it is the deficiency of this condition that has shaken the foundations of European spiritual edifice today.

I see in the English saint, John Henry Newman's theological pedagogy, the solution to Europe's faith predicament.

Let me explain myself. Suppose a man gets in class with the students, let us say, as a teacher and evangeliser, and becomes an expert in his material, and teaches his students academic concepts that enlighten, abstract and impersonal ideas that inspire. Or may be churns out doctrinal prescriptions and invites the students to commit them to memory. In our Christian schools you find that kind of thing today - where religious knowledge is just another subject to be learned and passed during examinations. But suppose this teacher never thinks to give himself a pause, to ponder and to wonder whether this knowledge has any concrete touch in his own soul, never pause to ponder whether to bring it down to the personal, whether to help his students understand what the teaching material means in their own lives; suppose this teacher gets into the rut of thoughtless routine, and does not ask himself whether the facts acquired will lead in the long run to the development or desolation of the community, in order to warn his students of impending danger – would such a man be called a outstanding catechist or teacher of the new evangelization, even if he were gifted with a tremendous teaching talent or with an intelligence sharp and powerful and was armed with a doctorate in theology?

My answer is: No. And saying no with me is one of the greatest authorities in theological education the world has ever seen - John Henry Newman.

For his part Newman decisively laid it down, without mincing words, that since "the heart is commonly reached, not through the reason, but through the imagination, by means of direct impressions, by the testimony of facts and events, by history, by description," those destined to be teachers of faith must credibly do so by personal influence and personal presence, for, "persons influence us, voices melt us, looks subdue us, deeds inflame us. Many a man will live and die upon a dogma: no man will be a martyr for a conclusion."[32] The person who thumbs the pages of Newman's writings does not fail to be charmed by his personal presence even in his books. For all his excellence in writing, Newman did not disdain the irreplaceable place of personal integrity, - and not lip service – in Christian holiness. He advised his soul in prayer: "Let me preach Thee without preaching, not by words but by my example, by the catching force, the sympathetic influence of what I do, the evident fullness of the love my heart bears to Thee!"[33] Pope Paul VI caps a memorable season by employing something similar to the just mentioned Newmanian superlative. Paul VI said that, "Modern man listens more willingly to witnesses than to teachers, and if he does listen to teachers, it is

---

[32] J. H. NEWMAN, *Grammar of Assent,* Longman Green and Co., London 1909, 92-93.
[33] J: H. NEWMAN, in *Totus Tuus*, "Blessed John Henry Newman"http://totus2us.com/vocation/blesseds/bl-john-henry-newman/

because they are witnesses." Newman describes this type of thing in a page of his *Grammar of Assent*: "I have no confidence, then in philosophers who…sit at home, and reach forward to distances which astonish us; but they hit without grasping, and are sometimes as confident about shadows as about realities. They have worked out by a calculation the lie of the country which they never saw, and mapped it by means of a gazeteer; and like blind men, though they can put a stranger on his way, they cannot walk straight themselves, and do not feel it quite their business to walk at all."[34]

What then are those outstanding evangelizing principles, guiding principles that flow from Newman's theological pedagogy which have an echo on the current spirit of New Evangelization? First of all, the epitaph John Henry Newman chose for his tombstone is the central message of all evangelizations: 'Ex umbris et imaginibus in veritatem' ('Out of shadows and images into the truth'). These words are more than the expression of Newman's entire life – they summarize the pilgrimage of each genuine Christian, battling each day to look for, to reach out and come upon the fullness of Truth that is Christ. To Newman, Christ was everything: "We do not hesitate to say …. that it really does arise from practical neglect of our Saviour."[35] Christ to him was Truth. This Truth was contained in the dogmas and revealed principles of the Church. So revealed truths were dynamic living thing. Newman's adoration of dogmas can hardly be regarded exaggerated. The striking delineations, remarkable modeling and classification of revealed truths are the garlands "set up in record of the victories of the Faith".[36] He calls the Athanasian creed "the war-song of faith", "a hymn of praise to the Eternal Trinity."[37] These revealed truths are ever "springing into life with inexhaustible fecundity".[38] They are ever gushing forth from the wounded side of Christ's Sacred Heart.

---

[34] J. H. NEWMAN, *Grammar of Assent*.
[35] Newman, Letter to John Keble, 27 August 1837; lxxxvii(oct. 1972) p. 701.
[36] J. H. NEWMAN, *Grammar of Assent*, (London: Longman Green and Co. 1909), 133.
[37] J. H. NEWMAN, *Parochial and Plain Sermons*, (London: Longman Green and Co. 1908), II 270.
[38] J. H. NEWMAN, *Grammar of Assent* (London: Longman Green and Co. 1909), 148.

And so dogma to him was truth. The challenge of the Church of today is to turn the heart of the modern faithful to the love again of Truth, of revealed truths, in this dispensation of new evangelization.

But to get to this truth there is need for another more important component. For us to reach the truth of things, Newman believed that we must search for it in all corners of the room, we must dig down to the beginnings and we must hunt higher up the heights. He would call it 'the enlargement of the mind' which involves,

> not merely in the passive reception into the mind of a number of ideas unknown to it, but in the mind's energetic and simultaneous action upon and towards and among those new ideas, which are rushing in upon it...And therefore a truly great intellect, ... such as the intellect of Aristotle, or of St. Thomas, or of Newton, or of Goethe, ... is one which takes a connected view of old and new, past and present, far and near, and which has an insight into the influence of all these one on another; without which there is no whole, and no centre.[39]

One of the ways today's Europe can fairly face itself, in enlarging its mind as Newman prescribes, is to do so by looking at its connection with other continents. The African angle is worth a thought.

The celebrated African novelist, Chinua Achebe, made some significant remarks about Africa and Europe. He named the geographical positioning of these two continents "joined together at a navel"; and he continues that "It is a great irony of history and geography that Africa, whose landmass is closer than any other to the mainland of Europe, should come to occupy in the European psychological disposition the farthest point of otherness, should indeed become Europe's very antithesis".[40] 'Joined together at a navel' Achebe christens the African-European location. Few European

---

[39] J. H. NEWMAN, *The Idea of a University*, 134.
[40] CHINUA ACHEBE, *The Education of a British-Protected Child*, New York, 2009, Alfred A. Knopt, 77.

theologians (if only there is any other) had so intimately seen Africa and Europe as joined together in a navel and had honored and spoken in high spirits about that persecuted continent as did John Henry Newman. Even as a European theologian, Newman's two most appealing theological stars – Augustine of Hippo and Athanasius of Alessandria - are all Africans. *Callista* is Newman's novel whose plot is in Africa (Tunisia). The novel's protagonist Callista is from the West(Greece). Peter and Paul the famed apostles, from the East, have carried the fresh faith from homeland and crossed to Rome. In the novel, they are already spoken of as examples and martyrs. The African saint, Bishop Cyprian evangelizes and baptizes Europe's Callista. More than a fictional work therefore, the novel *Callista* is a sermon illustration. It demonstrates the contribution of Africa to the evangelization of other parts of the world during the early period of the Church. So in one novel Newman connects the continents into one brotherhood. In that novel, the author touches on the African world, the Western world and the Eastern world – three inviolable historic continental positions. Newman has, whether we like it or not, come to stand for something much more than England or Europe. He is a symbol for the catholic side of the Church, a more intercontinental Catholic Church, which is best captured in the wise words of Pope Francis, that "the People of God is incarnate in the peoples of the earth, each of which has its own culture"[41].. This is the spirit which the New Evangelization encourages among its faithful around the globe – a looking at things from loftier perspectives, a broadening of our horizons because we are living, as never before, in intercultural times.

We come now to the most significant aspect of Newman's evangelizing process. It is that which is called Holiness. Evangelization, in the truest interpretation of the word, is holiness. Of course, one of Pope Francis's renown writings is dedicated to holiness with a modern face. In that work, he resonates so well with John Henry Newman's down-to-earth idea of holiness. Newman saw holiness as ordinary life lived perfectly: "If you ask me what you are to do

---

[41] FRANCIS, *Evangelii Gaudium*, 115.

in order to be perfect, I say, first – Do not lie in bed beyond the due time of rising; give your first thoughts to God; make a good visit to the Blessed Sacrament; say the Angelus devoutly; eat and drink to God's glory; say the Rosary well; be recollected; keep out bad thoughts; make your evening meditation well; examine yourself daily; go to bed in good time, and you are already perfect."[42] It means we are next door to eternity, that we are close to the dead, and that our ancestors are around, for according to Pope Francis "the saints now in God's presence preserve their bonds of love and communion with us".[43] John Henry Newman venerated values; he esteemed books; he admired the best in good and inspiring men and women. But he put holiness of life as the measure of all things. It was not just holiness, but holiness not fabricated. It was to be unconscious holiness, - what Newman calls holiness embodied in personal form, presence, the silent conduct of a holy man[44] Undoubtedly holiness is the lifeblood of Christian life but there shouldn't be any doubt if a saint is taken the wrong way because "the holier a man is, the less he is understood by men of the world."[45] Of course, God "wants us to be saints and not to settle for a bland and mediocre existence."[46] The surest way to persuade people to God is through unconscious holiness: "The attraction, exerted by unconscious holiness, is of an urgent and irresistible nature; it persuades the weak, the timid the wavering and the inquiring; it draws forth the affections and loyalty of all who are in a measure likeminded."[47] By this example, the disciple of Christ, the saint, the Christian of the new evangelization can help transform his faith-hostile and unchristian community into that spiritual public, the creation of which spiritual public should constitute the primary drive of his undertakings.

---

[42] J. H. NEWMAN, *Meditations and Devotions*, Christian Classics, Westminster, Md. 1975, p. 286.
[43] FRANCESCO, Apostolic Exortation, *Gaudete et Exsultate*, 19 March 2018, 4..
[44] J. H. NEWMAN, *Fifteen Sermons Preached before the University Of Oxford*, Longman Green and Co., London 1909, 91-92.
[45] J. H. NEWMAN, *Parochial and Plain Sermons*, vol. IV, 244.
[46] FRANCIS, Apostolic Exortation, *Gaudete et Exsultate*, 19 March 2018, 1.
[47] J. H. NEWMAN, *Fifteen Sermons Preached before the University Of Oxford*, Longman Green and Co., London 1909, 95.

In Newman one hardly exhausts the discovery of hot-button realities presented with accomplished accuracy. His theme tunes are so hypnotic that their freshness, their enthralling magical spell holds minds and hearts always captive. Take for instance the subject matter of conscience which I feel is one garden-fresh area for new evangelization. New Evangelization is education to maturity. Because it is that type of evangelization where its emphasis is the baptized and not the pagan, it concerns itself with making Christians complete Christians. This means especially that lay people can make decisions for themselves, can use their consciences and decide what to them is God's will in their lives. That is how Newman saw things and that is why he fought tooth and nail for the education and liberation of the laity in the Church. To him, conscience is "a consciousness of innocence and integrity."[48] The Church of the new evangelization especially that of Pope Francis' magisterium preaches the gospel of conscience in wonderful ways. He has opted for ripeness in faith. Newman once remarked:

> If either the Pope or the Queen demanded of me an 'Absolute Obedience', he or she would be transgressing the laws of human nature and human society. I give an absolute obedience to neither. Further, if ever this double allegiance pulled me in contrary ways (…), then I should decide according to the particular case, which is beyond all rule, and must be decided on its own merits.[49]

Francis has done this most especially in his *Amoris Laetitia*: "We also find it hard to make room for the consciences of the faithful, who very often respond as best they can to the Gospel amid their limitations, and are capable of carrying out their own discernment in complex situations".[50] He challenges priests and encourages marriage couples into Christian maturity. Newman and Francis teaches us that

---

[48] J. H. Newman, *PPS V*, cit., 238.
[49] J. H. NEWMAN, Diff II, cit., 243.
[50] FRANCIS, Apostolic Exhortation, *Amoris Laetitia*, 19 March 2016, 37.

conscience is a moral and authoritative critical sense; but they also firmly hold that conscience is a cerebral sentiment, an emotion, for it is "… something more than a moral sense; it is always, what the sense of the beautiful is only in certain cases; it is always emotional. No wonder then that it always implies what that sense only sometimes implies; that it always involves the recognition of a living object, towards which it is directed."[51] Because he is so universal on all-inclusive subjects like conscience, Newman gives meaning to the Church of the new evangelization and even today, the title of great is one that few will deny him.

One key area of interest in evangelization today is the role of the theologian. Newman was of the conviction that "religion cannot maintain its ground at all without theology. Sentiments, whether imaginative or emotional, falls back upon the intellect for its stay… and it is in this way that devotion falls back upon dogma."[52] It is individual theologians and not the Institutional Church, that have pioneered the inventiveness of faith, and been forerunners of the Catholic mind in the theological enterprise.[53] The individual genius of Augustine of Hippo, of Thomas Aquinas and today, of Newman of Birmingham, are the lights that have shone the way for the Church of their times and beyond.

Those who know him best know that it was in his personal letters – especially those to friends – that Newman's profound wisdom sparkled. He defined theology - in the finest words that define the subject of theology – as " like dancing on the tight rope some hundred feet above the ground. It is hard to keep from falling, and the fall is great. The questions are so subtle, the distinctions so

---

[51] J. H. Newman, AG, cit., 109-110.
[52] H. NEWMAN, *Grammar of Assent,* Longman Green and Co., London 1909, 121.
[53] See Newman "it is individuals and not the Holy See, that have taken the initiative, and given the lead to the Catholic mind, in theological inquiry."

fine, and critical jealous eyes so many."⁵⁴ To Newman the theological position of loyal opposition defines the true theologian. Of course, "Newman's theology is that of steadiness, dynamism and grace"⁵⁵ Theological inquiry is a minority body whose critical look at the body of Church content is responsible, useful and obliging. For this to be active, thinkers must mount the tight-rope to dare dangers and take risks, though endowed with intellectual humility and honesty. He held magisterium-incumbents for derision concerning theologizing because there was no theology if the theologian kept on repeating what popes had said and had no critical challenging nerve in the theological enterprise.

Since the depths of Truth are unfathomable, since God's grace is immeasurable, since the riches of beauty and goodness are inexhaustible, it follows that the genuine theologian must be a thorough researcher inquirer all his day. On these grounds Newman gave no quarter to mediocrity or a pandering to bigoted dogmatism:

> Our theological philosophers are like the old nurses who wrap the unhappy infant in swaddling bands or boards – put a lot of blankets over him – and shut the windows that not a breath of fresh air may come to his skin – as if he were not healthy enough to bear wind and water in due measures. They move in a

---

[54] *'The Letters and Diaries of John Henry Newman* (hereafter cited as LD) 22:215 (Newman to Bowles, April 16, 1866); the occasion for the letter was the appearance of his Letter to the Rev. E. B. Pusey, D.D., on his recent Eirencon (originally published in LondonLongmans, Green, Reader, and Dyer, 1866; later published in the second volume of Certain difficulties felt by Anglicans in Catholic teaching considered, London: Longmans, Green, and Co., 1885 and subsequently). In an earlier letter to Miss Bowles (1818-19049) Newman acknowledged the limitations of his reply to Pusey: "Don't expect much from my Pamphlet, which is at last through the Press. Pusey's work is on too many subjects, not to allow of a dozen answers—and since I am only giving one, every reader will be expecting one or other of the eleven which I don't give. Mine is only upon our belief concerning the Blessed Virgin." LD 22:128 (Newman to Bowles, January 18, 1866).

[55] Cfr. GERALD JUMBAM NYUYKONGMO, *A Laity who Know their Religion.*, Demdel Edition, 2018.

groove, and will not tolerate any one who does not move in the same.[56]

And so those uncharitable (in the name of orthodoxy) to new theological concepts of theologians of other continents or regions of the world, or those that put blankets here and there over theological debate or those who move in a groove, in one furrow of thought, in a theological single trench of mediocrity, must know they are doing untold damage to the blossoming of Christian thought. They should listen to Pope Francis that, "the theologian who is satisfied with his complete and conclusive thought is mediocre. The good theologian and philosopher has an open, that is, an incomplete, thought, always open to the *maius* of God and of the truth, always in development, according to the law that Saint Vincent of Lerins described in these words: *annis consolidetur, dilatetur tempore, sublimetur aetate*"[57] The goal of Europe's theologian today (and it seems to me, every theologian around the world) is to rehabilitate Christian thought in his present Christian-hostile ambient and doing so, to enlarge his mind with other worlds of reality hitherto unknown to him and combine standards of scholarship before unknown in Christian theology with attitudes critical of Church clericalism which have become likewise uncustomary.

According to the president of the Vatican Council for New Evangelization, Archbishop Rino Fisichella, New Evangelization is " the time for a new and mature apologetics of our faith, to offer hope to today's world"[58]. It has never been about the individual. It is about the naked, the captive, the destitute, the sick. The great thing about the Church of the New Evangelization is that it gives voice to the voiceless. Pope Francis arises as the embodiment of this radicalism of the gospel spirit, and through meditated actions has been the vocal sound of those who have even lost the strength to cry; has spoken for those poor around the globe under the terrible

---

[56] H. NEWMAN, Letters and Diary of John Henry Newman (LD). xxiv. 316.
[57] FRANCESCO, Apostolic Constitution, *Veritatis Gaudium*, 29 January 2018.
[58] RINO FISICHELLA, "We Need New Evangelizers", in *Year of Faith*, 09-08-2012, http://www.annusfidei.va/content/novaevangelizatio/en/news/09-08-2012.html

tyranny of a callous colonialism of the underprivileged, of a hyper-capitalistic market gone mad. The mandate of every true Christian on earth is to help the helpless, defend the unarmed, and speak for the powerless. The Christian principle sparkles when the poor have a place at the table, when the weak are strengthened and the unarmed are armed. Newman was voice of the voiceless in the way he spoke for the laity, and the way he stood against the tyranny of the Anglican faithful over the minority and bewildered Catholic of England. He enriched the poor of his time with the goods he manufactured best – his articles and books. With the poor laity who did not know their right from their left in the Church gone too clerical, he refined and enriched their minds and hearts with *On Consulting the Faithful in Matters of Doctrine*. With the poor English and Irish Catholics in England who found no place in English politics and among Anglican compatriots, he enriched them with his open letter to the Duke of Norfolk and *Lectures on the Position of Catholics in England*. To the unenlightened Ireland about university studies he enriched them with *The Idea of a University*. When the Catholic Church's clergy celibacy was attacked by a fierce English writer, Newman singled out to bear the burden of so outrageous a charge, demanded that the author, the Rev. Charles Kingsley, either give evidence or surrender. What ensued for the defense of the Church and himself was the production of a remarkable record of self-disclosure baptized *Apologia Pro Vita Sua*, which has become a Christian classic. The work was a triumph not only for Newman but for the entire Roman Catholic Church in England. Yet it would be shortsightedness to see the success of this writing only from that standpoint. It was a work that manifested the fighting spirit of a man who did not want to see the poor suffer for nothing. The Catholic Church was the poor person who was under pangs of pain in Anglican-infested Britain. Newman took his pen up out also of pity for this oppressed and helpless body of Christ in a hyper-critical and arrogant England.

"I have a work to do in England", Newman remarked when he was about to leave Italy (Sicily) and return home, and so he had. But the work would turn out to be for the whole Catholic Church, a work that would live forever, a work that is leading him to the high altars of canonization come October. In the spirit of his famous hymn 'Lead Kindly Light' composed in Italy, and "amid the encircling gloom" of pedagogical and pastoral mediocrity in the Church, Newman abidingly provided a " kindly light" in the new evangelization with his edifying personal presence in the Church.

Chapter Three

NEWMAN AND THE AFRICAN WAY

To a typical African, faith like a key has no intentions. Its intentions are that it opens the door; there is no cunning ploy in his faith. The largely established verdict on 21st century Christian - that his obsessive liberal character eclipses the obvious significance of faith – is one that few wish to dispute. Already, the very phrase 'liberalism in religion' was used by John Henry Newman to denote a uniquely modern great *apostasia* that essentially has been hunting down community life and eternal principles. As with concepts so with consequences and the consequence Newman predicted, was infidelity not only to the eternal principles but also to God. I tumbled recently on a statement made by Cardinal Francis George of Chicago. He was talking about the future of the Church: "I expect to die in bed, my successor will die in prison and his successor will die a martyr in the public square. His successor will pick up the shards of a ruined society and slowly help rebuild civilization, as the Church has done so often in human history".[59]

To those who know how to read the signs of the times, the fear expressed by the Cardinal is understood. The metaphor of death here is an astonishing one. It speaks of life as death and vice versa, and I am most concerned at the fact that, to my mind, accent to God is what crosses the divide between death and life. Obvious to me then is

---

[59] FRANCIS GEORGE, in TIM DRAKE "Cardinal George: The Myth and Reality of 'I'll Die in My Bed'", 24 October, 2012, *National Catholic Register*, http://www.ncregister.com/blog/tim-drake/the-myth-and-the-reality-of-ill-die-in-my-bed

not whether one finds himself in the most confortable generation, or in the generation of " martyr in public square" or the generation that "will pick up the shards of a ruined society". What is most significant is that one holds a steadfast faith. And therefore, what is faith? The simple story of two couples would help us. A man and a woman stood holding hands at the mountainside. For a time, the only sound was the deafening silence and whistles of birds. Then the man asked, "What makes you frightened ?" She responded: "I want to marry you more than anything on earth. But I keep fearing you will abandon me on the way…" Her eyes fell to the ground. "Just like your dad left your mom?" he asked gently. Hesitantly, she nodded.

"Don't you trust me?" he asked.

"I do," she interjected. "You are the most responsible man I have come across." She stopped, then dejectedly whispered, "But I'm afraid that you'll realize that I'm not what you really want."

He clasped her hands more resolutely and assured her: " We have been friends, best friends since our teens. I am used to your mistakes and you mine. But our love has not waned. It is still as fresh as it was. You have been my choice and I have no one else like you. "

"I do trust you," she whispered lovingly, "I only desire to know how to believe in you."

In my country we do not peer through the binoculars of logic and argument in order to decode faith. When we believe, it is not for a particular reason. We believe in my homeland simply because for many reasons there is no other reason than to believe. Belief is self-contained and stands alone. But who tells you that we don't go for evidence? who tells you that my people do not assent to what they know is right and just? who tells you that we do not study nature and its secrets in order to believe well? Faith is this simple engaging approach to a pedagogic delineation of the workings of religious belief, the most fascinating, the most universal, and therefore the most Catholic. Catholic because it touches on the cord of simple believing faith, the way of belief of the common man out there.

Visiting Africa today, you can be smitten by one or both of two thoughts. The first of these is the robust and ongoing mark of Western and Islamic colonialism. The second is the elemental, unchanging, gigantic integrity of native Africa. It is, I always find, the traces of the second which make you appreciate the ruthlessness of the first. "Nobody can teach me who I am." Achebe underscores, "You can describe parts of me, but who I am – and what I need – is something I have to find out myself." True believing faith in its warm, strange and peculiar character dictates unto the subject a raw intimacy. It tells you no one can teach you well except you. Belief in God is first of all belief in self, in personal possibilities. It is how to stand on your own feet and call God by His personal name.

There is a Creation myth among our people that human beings once made up their mind to send an emissary to Nyuy, the supreme god, if the dead could be permitted to come back to life. As their envoy, they chose a chameleon. But the chameleon delayed, and a tortoise, which had been eavesdropping, reached Nyuy first. Wanting to punish man, the tortoise reversed the request, and told Nyuy that after death men did not want to return to the world. God said that he would do as they wished, and when the tortoise arrived with the true message he refused to change his mind. Thus, men may be born again, but only in a different form.

The lesson of this little story is the lesson of faith. There is danger in thinking that you can believe for another person. With God there is no delegation. You do it yourself. The road of faith is an unbeaten path that only the person in question can travel. If you allow it to others, the fate of man in the story above would be yours. Belief is rootedness inside you. It tells you to tell your own story. It challenges your roots and breaks earth for them to grow looking heavenward. So we are not afraid to be saints because the thing is us.

I have seen in my time thousands of crafts workers, street sweepers and blue-collar workers, intelligent and gladder than university chairs and rectors. Yet again, see how these poor and underprivileged men and women who get the heat of the sun in daily tedious doings. They know neither Wole Soyinka nor Bill Gates and yet from them life flows to the world and God speaks to them in their simplicity and ordinariness, more than any of the highfaluting scholars and scientists today. God master of the universe is master of life. He created us freely and wants us to freely live. The awareness that we are next door to eternity, that we are one in heart with the dead, that our ancestors are around and that heaven is a possibility, urges us on to redouble our efforts and live believing and fulfilled lives.

What the almost four decades of my lifespan have brought, undeniably, has been the speediest age of technological transformation ever observed; and yet so much misery, injustice and want stares us everywhere in the face. "The poor are always with you.", the words of Christ, in our time are troublingly true. Undeniably, today, the global gap between the rich and the poor is scandalizing. The human predicament is changing, in many ways, for the worst. Yet, there is still life and joy as antithesis of tears and lamentation. There is still compassion on earth. Men and women fall in love. Thank God, too, these affirmations have not changed. As you would imagine, and for the believer, God still reigns. Indeed, whether as Elijah saw, in the bustle of earthquake and fire or the mystery of cyber wonders, or the cacophony of phone call center or the jangling of the supermarket, God still reigns - as present in those rattling spaces as he is in the still small voice of conscience. And thus, the call of evangelization, everywhere.

The afternoon of the cross of faith. It was one of those few afternoons where people feel that justice, faith and love are one. When you have gone through pain, felt stifled, victimized, discriminated against, and rubbished by circumstances. Now when you imagine this and feel in your bone a desperation so deep and unfair, if you pray, and sincerely be confident that there is a Higher Power that can turn things around, your heart will puff out one of the universe's most powerful feelings: Belief.

I am beginning to think that maybe this world is the hell of my great great great grandparents. I won't be surprised if this thought resonates with the many Africans whom life has become a hell of great many conundrums bastardising the whole future of their future generations. Experience is the greatest teacher. Another word for experience is history and another word for history is suffering. Many people are molded by suffering and a good many too are destroyed by that type of suffering that breaks the back, the annihilating side of history. Someone says, "I don't get involved, I am not practicing,

I don't care about experience". Experiences are part of the practice of faith, of assenting and trusting. Experience brings us closer to the reality of affirming reality and people. Until an English poet said the world is a stage. It is true but I add that that stage is full of people who dislike the rehearsals that prepare each person for a better performance on stage. That rehearsal is experience and once you rehearse, the magic is that you perform well in this world stage Thus the message of the power of experience. It takes a great deal of courage to experience and still to belief. Assenting to the God idea with the intimacy of experience is belief indeed. Belief has no logic to its form. Its logic is: Belief. Belief is being yourself. It is knowing yourself. We dig into our being and see what we can do best, what we can contribute to humanity. We do because we are happy and we make life happy because we do what makes us and others happy. God "wants us to be saints and not to settle for a bland and mediocre existence."[60] Here, belief is a practical thing. It is concreteness of life. It is not lived in books and faced in sanctuaries. it is out there with people, in the marketplace in the office in the playground. The primitive community of Christians of the first century in Jerusalem are described in the Acts of the Apostles as: a multitude of those who having become believers had one mind, one soul and one heart. With exemplary courage gave testimony to the resurrection of Jesus, pulling their resources together and no one among them was poor. All enjoyed a great heavenly favor. They are a model for every Christian community, every believing community. This is the idea of life God has put before us for our gaze. We today are also called to be one mind, one heart, and one soul, thus witnessing to the resurrection of Christ by sharing our lives and our goods, loving each one as God has loved us. This is the only testimony that a community is Christian.

It is a melancholy truth that a child-like man is a man of faith. He is one who, even in old age, is in school. Everlasting chances are given him because he never, like Jacob, stops playing with God. Belief as an eternal principle allows us to see the ancient times more intimately than is possible in a Church history book. But, just as

---

[60] FRANCIS, Apostolic Exortation, *Gaudete et Exsultate*, 19 March 2018, 1.

importantly, it allows us to compare the day-to-day living of yesterday with that of today. Belief in God is at the heart of what makes me me. I believe that it doesn't matters how much I believe, nor how far I can go. The assent to God's omnipotence is what matters to me this here moment. This faith to me is not an invention. It is life. It is my heartbeat. I understand because I come from a place where spirituality is in our DNA. I believe in God because he created all, and he true to all. African Traditional Religion (ATR), like any other serious world religion, is simply unstoppable! The more its illuminations are thought to be turned down, the greater its light intensifies, and the sunnier it sparkles. But black Africa are a very unique people. Their religion is not just simply tolerant, it is gifted in acceptance - the attitude of living and allowing others space to live. It is knowledge born of the heart, the kind of knowledge John speaks about: "But you have been anointed by the Holy One, and have all received knowledge" (1 John 2:20). This knowing passes into our instincts, ligaments, impulses. It becomes a habit, an attitude, it is so private and personal that it is not able to be explained except from some intimate whisperings without any meaning to the ordinary carnal bystander.

Faith is tangible and contemporary. Oh the urgency of faith that animated my soul when the affliction of our Ambazonian people was leading towards something like a genocide. At that point in time, I considered the writing of each essay on the predicament as the equivalent of saying Mass. I boasted at that moment, and rightly so, of only two corners of mankind I was certain of enlightening, and that was myself and my homeland. That faith has taught me that the most prized part of knowledge that be, is the ability to compel me do the things I must do, at the time I want it done, whether they like it or not.

We don't strain too much if we make mistakes, if we fall on mud – because we do not idolize cleanliness and make it a god. We brazenly avow with Teresa of Calcutta: "Yes, I have many human faults and failures… But God bends down and uses us, you and me, to be his love and his compassion in the world; he bears our sins, our troubles and our faults. He depends on us to love the world and to show how much he loves it". Belief is the lifeblood of life in my homeland because it is normal to believe.

Either you recapture hope or plunge into despair. What is the most beautiful thing I get back when I make a desert all about me? Myself. Ourselves, I, you, we are the most beautiful gift to us. There is no formula or way of believing. You leant that you fell in love when you were already comforted in a woman's laps. Faith is falling in love and not knowing how it happened. You can't define faith. It opens the heart, washes the soul, exercises the frame of mind and moistens the feelings; so believe. To understanding what is going on in this desert of our hearts and in the world, we need to reflect on two things. One is to know what people truly believe. The other is what they do with what they believe in. It is easy to dismiss colonialists as looters, not least because they are. But they have an acute sense of one thing: belief. They created their trade on others' resources in the assuring corridors of faith in their homeland and in the determination to pinch so much and so well that as they impoverish others, they enriched themselves.

There is some chaos in belief. Knowledge and reason are not enough for evidence of God's existence. Logic is good. Its bearings are real instruments to train the mind and make decisions. But it is not in logic that the full assent of faith is. Concrete living, practical conviction is already belief; for we believe well by doing belief.

People today, in the Church or outside, are hungry for depth. This desire to open hearts up to people outside limited religious culture is what inspires proclamation and evangelization. There was never any conversion without the hearts of faithful going out to embrace the lonely, the stranger and the heretic. And therefore, there is something that touches a deeper nerve, whether we are aware of it or not, and it is the African vision of communal life, and the culture's penetrating sense of belonging. I delve into the spirit of the belief system of my people today because I believe with that fine African storyteller of Nigerian descent Chinua Achebe that "Every generation must recognize and embrace the task it is peculiarly designed by history and by providence to perform." In reality a person's way of believing would be a media circus unless it causes the person to realize that there is a communal dimension to the responsibility of faith. What is here is on the subject matter of belief – the language of belief. To show how concrete faith is lived and how faith blossoms. To show how natural ways of thinking helps us to believe in God. To simply remind me and others of the simple faith of my Cameroonian old grand mothers who have never seen the four walls of school, who believe just like me and whose crude chaotic way of believing is altogether belief. The writing may be couched in polished language, it may be decked with fine scholarly phrases but those phrases express the habits of simple faithful who believe and whose belief can't be reduced to logic and hard-dry philosophical evidences.

Once accent is properly rooted in its unique perspective, it is seen to go beyond that perspective and speak to the contemporary Church. The beauty of being Catholic is that your faith crosses the divide between the personal and the universal, the home and the foreign. No doubt Pope Francis has recently met tough times simply because he takes the Church back not only to Ancient times, but also to his homeland. One's identity should never get missing in what one does. To show how we can believe with the certainty of homeland, a certainty that owns a large-heartedness of accommodating other lands and climes.

The word faith is an untidy tangled word. The great Christian thinker of the 11th century, Anselm of Canterbury, summarized this in three words "faith seeking understanding". The cultivation of the mind and the intellectual responsibility of using that mind to know truth is typically Christian. Christianity honors the intellectual duty. The faith that is Christian is one that has gone through discernment, leads to responsibility and commits itself to hold on even against the winds of time. It is the one thing Thomas the Apostle teaches us in his profession of faith. Thomas can't believe Jesus is risen from the dead. He is a practical man. He saw Jesus die, buried in his grave: but how is that possible? Thomas won't believe, but he won't leave. He stays in the community, and that is what would save him. This because in the community of apostles Jesus returns and comes just to meet him, to get him identify, to get rid of the darkness in his heart and to offer him the light of a great faith. "Don't be unbelieving, but believe. Put here you hand, touch the wounds, see that it is really me".

"My Lord and my God": so Thomas enters in the certitude of that faith that he will not abandon anymore and for which he will commit to death all his life. The joy of belief explodes in the heart of the apostle.

The apostles locked up themselves because of fear. Fear is the paralysis of life. Only meetings open the future and starts time running afresh. Jesus knows this very well, and therefore turns to Thomas: Put your finger here. Christ had taught Thomas interior freedom, gave him courage, and instilled in him the love of humanity. To ennoble him the more, he rebukes him a little, but softly, as friends would normally do to each other: do not be unbelieving....he respects his times and instead of imposing, he proposes: put, watch, touch. And Thomas puts, watches and touches.

But let's be clear about this. Thomas symbolizes not only the Christian in crisis, he embodies the Christian virtue of belief, concrete tangible belief. He is the one who utters the highest and most moving profession of faith: My Lord and my God!

Thomas is the protagonist of our story today. He reminds me of a fundamental fact: that Jesus is not an invention, a fairy tale and least of all a projection of my desires. There is a hole in his hands and another on his chest, where a hand can enter!

Thank you Thomas, because I need to know that Jesus is not fiction or fantasy. Because I know now that belief in Him is neither mere theological disputations nor logic argumentations. I need to know, see, touch and feel. I need to experience it myself in me and by me. Thus in the hand of Thomas are my hands. That in the patient and lengthening experience of Thomas's 'language of assent', is my own language of assent. And that having witnessed this, having discovered my language of belief, I, in this cast-iron certainty of my assent can now explode with Thomas the Apostle: "my Lord and my God!". Thomas was African in so doing.

Chapter Four

CONSPIRATIO BETWEEN LAITY AND CLERGY

Thinking of a suitable image to celebrate the life of the man I have had three nerve-racking years contemplating his thought and etching a thesis out of the material pondered upon, I was initially drawn to a metaphor of a bicycle. I like to compare the Church to a stable bicycle whose wheels are kept spinning by the exploits of the likes of John Henry Newman. Should that forward propelling motion slow down as a result of a paucity of such Church thinkers, the pillars that define the Institution would begin to stagger. It would not be possible to enjoy theology from a time remote from your own, or from a culture overwhelmingly unlike yours, unless the theology share some mutual emotional ground and some deep pool of beliefs, with you. I feel as a Southern Cameroonian, that emotion and pool, each time I thumb the pages of the works of Newman the Englishman. By drawing on his intimate life experiences and the unfathomable reservoir of Church wisdom, an accomplishment like the work of John Henry Newman is as fresh as if it had been realized yesterday, and of course, such a theological contribution enjoys the power to cross the continents and the centuries.

When Ambrose the bishop of Milan welcomed and baptized a starry-eyed African philosopher from Algeria, little did he know he was preparing a bishop and one of the most important Church thinkers in the universal Church in the person of Augustine of Hippo. When Fr Dominic Barberi welcomed and baptized a fanatical Anglican scholar in the Catholic Church in the name of John Henry

Newman, little did he know he was preparing the catalyst of an Ecumenical Council held a century after, in his own home country Italy(Vatican II).

Callista is Newman's novel whose plot is in Tunisia (Africa). The novel's young and beautiful protagonist Callista is from Greece(Europe) and a pagan. The worldview is that of imperial Rome. The apostles Peter and Paul have carried the new faith from their homeland in the Middle-East and have crossed to Rome. In the novel, they are already spoken of as examples and martyrs in this Rome. So in one novel Newman connects the continents into one brotherhood. In that novel, the author touches on the African world, the Western world and the Eastern world – three inviolable historic continental positions. The setting of his *Callista* in Africa is indicative of his fondness for the homeland of his theological idols Athanasius and Augustine. Africa is therefore central to Newman's thought pattern. So Newman has, whether we like it or not, come to stand for something much more than England or Europe. He is a symbol for the catholic side of the Church, a more intercontinental Catholic Church. That is how he will be doctor of the universal Church.

Before I made the choice of my doctoral thesis from Newman, I had visited this Via Aurelia Newman library several times during the earlier two years of my licentiate studies, not for any dissertational studies, but to enrich my personal life with Newmanian ideas. Newman didn't therefore come to me accidentally.

I had all my schooling in the educational system of the former British Southern Cameroons. And I was fortunate to be groomed by parents who were Catholic school teachers. My father's humble library had the whole collection of the books of the celebrated Cameroonian scholar Dr. Bernard Fonlon who was such a Newman devotee that would spice his works with long extracts from Newman. I was then (since childhood) a voracious reader of this Cameroonian scholar and the more I read his books the more I admired Newman his idol. Then when I was admitted for studies to the priesthood in the St. Thomas Aquinas' major seminary Bambui Cameroon, its rich library that contained Newman's main works was a great feast for me.

This favorable background probably explains why my first encounter with the Newman library in Rome was a hypnotizing experience.

My generation in Africa, the post-colonial generation, has grown often reading the literature of writers (religious writers sometimes) of the territories of our former colonial masters with care, sometimes taking it with a pinch of salt ideas that speak condescendingly about an Africa we should know better than them. This because the present generation of emerging Africa is very sensitive to the type of patronizing attitudes their grandparents went through in the hands of colonial masters. You should know by now that my homeland, the Southern Cameroons, was a British colony. Yet, a major aspect of my discovery was to see (and what comfort it gave me!) that J. H. Newman was neither an abnormality nor was he likely to be a flash in the pan. My study of him has given me reason to trust the strange and the peculiar. It has made me to be flexible, to accommodate new ideas and to listen to other cultures and other voices like his. Newman's voice articulates itself always with compassion for suffering humanity, never pandering to theological imperialism or religious empire-building.

I went to Newman therefore, not because he was an English man. I went to him because Newman had made me realize with Terence(that great Roman poet of African descent) that as "I am human, … nothing human is alien to me."

The unacceptable position of the laity in Catholic England and Catholic Ireland of Newman's time was predominantly similar to Cameroon's contemporary Catholic climate. It is this deplorable condition of lay ignorance back home that inspired me to put pen to paper. Unfortunately as we now know, Church ignorance among the laity today is not exclusively Cameroonian - it cuts across national and continental lines. I do not need to remind my audience of what for example is happening in the German Catholic Church today, where the simple straight-forward definition of the Most Holy Sacrament of the Eucharist is sadly becoming a hydra-headed difficulty, not only to the German laity but also among some German Catholic clergy! And if gold should rust what would iron do. The Church really has work – work against this abysmal lack of knowledge of simple but fundamental theological questions, this folly raising its ugly head around the globe today.

I have come, after this long study of Newman on the education of the laity, to form certain convictions. One of them is that Christ's lay faithful people are the conscience of the Church. They are the voice of God in the Church to be listened to and consulted when making serious ecclesial decisions. But that conscience (the laity) must be formed. It is thanks to the importance of this formation that the study of my book *A Laity who Know their Religion* is inescapable in our time. The laity is to the Church what the pulse of the heart is to man and what the barometer is to the measuring of the atmospheric pressure. You must contact your heart often to know the state of the being of your whole corpus. The pulse of the heart is the heart itself, for without the pulse there is no life, and therefore without the laity the world is devoid of the living organism that is the Church. This fundamental ecclesial principle has stumble upon difficulties of accommodation in the Church for some past centuries. And each time and anywhere a local church has not accommodated this spirit, it has in such times betrayed the cause of the Church of Christ. But such laity if they are true to their calling must be an informed laity, for in the engaging words of Hermann Geissler in the Foreword to *A Laity who Know their Religion*, "Newman's prophecy that uneducated Christians will be prey either to indifference or to superstition has, unfortunately, in our time turned out to be troublingly true". So the Church has work to do - the work of educating its uneducated Christians and there are millions of them out there. I am convinced that that is the abiding mission of the Pontifical Council of New Evangelization today. The role of our Shepherds – Pope and Bishops – can never be overemphasized. They are essentially the preservers of the faith, and as leaders, we owe them respect. Yet, every Christian, both lay and clergy, is king, prophet and priest, thus, the burning need for a new *conspiratio* of the clergy and the laity in the noble mission of evangelization today.

Perhaps, the one feat Newman each time seeks to accomplish is the struggle to see things really as they are. In *The Idea of a University*, he invented the catchphrase "enlargement of mind". He understood by this, a "power of viewing many things at once as one whole, of referring them severally to their true place in the universal system, of understanding their respective values, and determining their mutual dependence."[61] What he teaches us here, is what Edith Stein portrayed in fine phrase, "all who seek truth seek God, whether this is clear to them or not".[62] A contrary spirit to this - establishes Pope Francis - is damaging to the Gospel: "A person who thinks only about building walls, wherever they may be, and not building bridges, is not Christian. This is not in the Gospel."[63] It is the honest opening of mind to Catholic ideas (when he was Anglican) that brought Newman to the Catholic Church. And as Catholic he says it is not the Catholic Church that made him Catholic, but the Anglican Oxford that schooled him to appreciate the Catholic spirit.

A pastor like Newman who enlarges his mind would open his heart to lay people, to strangers, to pagans, to people of all professions. Newman thus was of the conviction that all knowledge (divine knowledge also) had common ground, some eternal principles shared by all humanity, ideas which cut across theological, philosophical and scientific lines. In Christian parlance he sometimes called them revealed truths. It is thanks to this background that he appreciates the Catholic Magisterium and its time-honored tradition that has assumed the role of defender of these eternal principles from generation to generation.

In Newman one hardly exhausts the discovery of ideas in one or two readings. His themes are so spellbinding that the more we feel we already know, the more fresh, startling and original they become. Take for instance the subject matter of conscience. Newman is not the first to have expounded on the theme of conscience, but he does it in such a way that the thing encapsulates the whole universal and wrings through in every human ear. That is why I am charmed by an altogether new invigorating idea each time I read this man.

---

[61] J. H. NEWMAN, *The Idea of a University*, Discourse 6.
[62] EDITHSTEIN, *Quotable Quotes*, https://www.goodreads.com/quotes/7120820-all-those-who-seek-truth-seek-god-whether-this-is.
[63] POPE FRANCIS, During his *in-flight news conference from Mexico to Rome*, (February 18, 2016).

In these days of new evangelization, the entry of the term "inculturation" in the theological enterprise can be likened to the proverbial pebble thrown into a sea: it has sent waves all over the Christian globe and with such speed that has carried along also the debris of misinterpretations. But the term itself (inclulturation) is a wonderful one. It brings out the uniqueness of each one of us, and the celebration of that uniqueness. Solo cum Solo. Newman celebrated his Englishness with pride and without any apology. What then has this Englishness for the universal Church? It must be said that Newman's originality in the universal Church is to have employed on the theology of the Roman Catholic Church, that concreteness, that realism, that pragmatism and that common sense – his Anglican heritage - typical of the Anglo-Saxon world. In Newman's robust Englishness in theology we find an inculturated theologian, the prophetic voice of the new evangelization which continues to speak with powerful urgency today. In him, we see a religious thinker wholly ready for the business of enriching the universal Church with variety and beauty.

Newman believed that Rome was the religious centre of the world. Rome "is the religious centre of millions all over the earth, who care nothing for the Romans who happen to live there, and much for the martyred Apostles who so long have lain buried there; and its claim to have an integral place in the very idea of Catholicity is recognized not only by Catholics, but by the whole world."[64] Newman was that universal, but he adored his uniqueness, his English identity. This personal character as well as the universal temperament of Newman interrogates the Church of today: can we evangelize with a multicultural consciousness and still be the one true Catholic and apostolic Church? No serious thinker of the Church ever lost his uniqueness and identity. Thanks to this personal character within the context of his inculturating Englishness, Newman's place in the Missio ad Gentes is preserved.

The situation of Newman's England was similar to ours today because it was also a missionary territory for the *propaganda fide*. I

---

[64] J. H. NEWMAN, "The Pope and the Revolution", in *Sermons Preached on Various Occasions*, Vol. 4, 40.

did my license in moral theology in the Pontifical Urban university and one of my joys was to know that the great Newman had passed in that institution. He, the new Catholic convert came to the eternal city in the manner some of us came – from mission territories for theological studies. That is why I make no apologies when I speak about Newman and inculturation. In the spirit of John Paul II's *Ecclesia in Africa*, evangelization and inculturation are not incompatible. At the very core of his inculturating spirit, Newman doesn't lose his interior call of the universal and of history as captured so impressively in his masterpiece *An Essay on the Development of the Doctrine of the Church*. This interior call to the universal could not be lost because even in that Englishness, was the universal. That is why it resonates with me a Cameroonian.

Newman is now a global character; not merely an English man, related just to the Victorian age and with some matters within the Catholic Church in England. One reason he has become a global household name is his theological harvest. The second reason is his holiness. One other reason that sustains the first and second reasons is the power the English language wields today in the world. Thanks to the great transnational evangelizing spirit of largely Irish Catholic missionaries of the 19th and 20th centuries, Catholicism has deep roots in all English speaking nations. Great and large nations of the world like the USA, Nigeria, India, Australia, the Philippines, South Korea (just to name a few) have become massively significant in the Catholic world stage. The three years I had this study on Newman, here in Rome, I encountered many student-friends in the Via Aurelia Newman Library in Rome and in other pontifical libraries, friends who were also doing research and writing on Newman. So Newman is hot cake today also because English today is world language.

Since the days of Newman to ours, the Church has been under attack from the perils of religious liberalism as well as the hazards of ultra-traditionalism. In Newman's own words, "the trials which lie before us would appal and make dizzy even such courageous hearts as St. Athanasius, St. Gregory I, or St. Gregory VII. And they would confess that, dark as the prospect of their own day was to them severally, ours has a darkness different in kind from any that has been before."⁶⁵ We are the generation that can make a difference by turning it all around. We have been given a great gift today, the gift of holy and outstanding combatants like John Henry Cardinal Newman. This will be accomplished with the armor of solid theological education, especially the education of the laity.

I feel so honored to have had this chance to write about such a gigantic character, one whose standing is second to none in the field of the theological education of the Christian. The inaccessibility of Newman's ideas today is a pity to mankind. The greatest service we would do Newman is that his ideas should not keep on circulating only around academics. Newman was a man of the people because he championed the theological formation of the god-forsaken poor, the common man, the laity of his time. And therefore, Pope Francis' position that the poor and underprivileged are the "treasures of the Church,"⁶⁶ is quintessentially Newman. Let's not lose heart, because if we pause and reflect, we would see the solutions to the great many spiritual conundrums we face today in this simple, saintly and sagacious Englishman. Go get your copy of *A Laity Who Know their Religion*. The book is one of such Newman responses to these spiritual and moral tragedies of our time.

In brief, what I am saying is that Newman encouraged us to look inward, to pay attention to our consciences. An interior look and attention to the still small voice in us, enables us to see the objective and the universal in ways that we can never imagine. What I have also highlighted using the novel *Callista* for illustration is the universal touch of Newman – a man who saw the Church from a multi-continental, multifaceted dimension. So Newman is not just the property of Europe. In fact we Africans claim him more than any other continent because his theological idols were in fact all Africans: Athanasius and Augustine. I have also endeavored in this presentation to put Newman in context, the context of the Anglo-Saxon worldview, underlining his Englishness and showing how

---

[65] J. H. NEWMAN, "The Infidelity of the Future" (1973), in *Faith and Prejudice and other Sermons*, 116 – 124.

[66] POPE FRANCIS, *Wednesday Meeting with a Group of Poor and Disabled Pilgrims*, July 6, 2016.

in that Englishness is the universal. The fundamental issue here is that theology is not the exclusive métier of the clergy. This helps us to conclude that for the Church to be true to the intention of her Maker and her Spouse Jesus Christ, she must engage both the laity and the clergy in the study of the theology of the Church. It is the vigilant balancing of both the right of the laity to participate fully in the Church and have it as their own home, and the maintaining of the prerogative of the clergy to be able to lead the Church with humility that Newman stands out in this book as a Christian thinker, a theologian worthy of admiration.

CHAPTER FIVE

THE ENLARGEMENT OF THE MIND

"She [the Church] fears no knowledge, but she purifies all, she represses no element of our nature, but cultivates the whole"[67]

J. H. Newman

No concept of education has yet been tried today for humanity's renaissance which promises so much and is capable of so much for the enduring well-being of the world as the principle of intercultural pedagogy. The idea upon which Interculturalism is established has thus far stood the test. It is a philosophy with confident concrete consequences which everyone who is earnest in the desire for humanity's rebirth must admit, and which no one in our time, however hostile to humankind, will energetically compete against. Possibly, few things about the study of man are more misleading than cataloguing. Are you documented? Where are you *really* from? But you are not like us? You must find it really emancipating to live here? Is our culture not better than theirs? Your own face looks quite like you originate from the ape? Are you already part of the civilized world? They look more like barbarians, don't they? Conversations about such interrogations can fatigue all but xenophobes. And so much rests on the standpoint of the inquirer as well as the person

---

[67] J. H. NEWMAN, *The Idea of a University*, (London: Longmans, Green, and Co., 1907), 234.

and the matter addressed. With the consciousness that all people are images of God, the realization that the world has become a global village, the mindfulness that all people are born equal in dignity, in fact, with the unflinching conviction of "following Jesus Christ, who has torn down the hostile wall dividing Jews from gentiles, thereby inviting the community in him to work toward intercultural peace as part of its fidelity to the gospel" [68], a plainspoken Christian witness against the aforementioned throbbing interrogations is, I suppose, the most appropriate witness to all that is Christian humanism in our times.

Intercultural pedagogy? In this wide-ranging academic discipline, we are ready to draw on Newman for culture and theology. His influence on Christian education today is evident - a man who before now had seen Catholicism as the embodiment of Interculturalism, for it was his conviction that "the Church has ever appealed and deferred to witnesses and authorities external to herself, in those matters in which she thought they had means of forming a judgment: and that on the principle, *Cuique in arte sua credendum.*"[69] Whether pagan literature, whether pagan philosophy, whether pagan wisdom, Newman believed the Church has always epitomized cultural encounter with variegated cultures in even pagan and protestant folklore:

> She (the Church) has even used unbelievers and pagans in evidence of her truth, as far as their testimony went. She avails herself of scholars, critics, and antiquarians, who are not of her communion. She has worded her theological teaching in the phraseology of Aristotle; Aquila, Symmachus, Theodotion, Origen, Eusebius, and Apollinaris, all more or less heterodox, have supplied materials for primitive exegetics. St. Cyprian called Tertullian his master; {7} St. Augustin refers to Ticonius; Bossuet,

---

[68] J. P. ASHWORTH, "Who are our People? Toward a Christian Witness against Borders", in *Modern Theology* 34 (2018), 518.
[69] J. H. NEWMAN, *The Idea of a University*, 6.

in modern times, complimented the labours of the Anglican Bull; the Benedictine editors of the Fathers are familiar with the labours of Fell, Ussher, Pearson, and Beveridge. Pope Benedict XIV cites according to the occasion the works of Protestants without reserve, and the late French collection of Christian Apologists contains the writings of Locke, Burnet, Tillotson, and Paley. If, then, I come forward in any degree as borrowing the views of certain Protestant schools on the point which is to be discussed, I do so, Gentlemen, as believing, first, that the Catholic Church has ever, in the plenitude of her divine illumination, made use of whatever truth or wisdom she has found in their teaching or their measures; and next, that in particular places or times her children are likely to profit from external suggestions or lessons, which have not been provided for them by herself.[70]

Thanks to this broadmindedness of a thinker, thanks to his perennial principles on intercultural pedagogy, we shall model a mode of critical discourse long needed. Doubtless, John Henry Newman will be an obliging and enlightening figure on this vital topic. Two of his most emblematic teachings — on enlargement of the mind and on personal influence — would be suggested by this essay and be treated in detail in the light of intercultural pedagogy.

I must make a clean breast from the start that I have neither the aspiration nor the aptitude to apply myself to this exercise with the tools of sociological or anthropological penetration but do so more modestly in the style of an educationist highlighting the compelling example of John Henry Newman and riveting my reader's gaze on his enduring intercultural ecclesial principles. We are talking about a man who believed that the Church was the home, not of a tribe, not of a country, not of a continent, but that Christianity was at home with every people, every culture, every civilization, every race; because Christianity, " is in its idea an announcement, a preaching; it is the

---

[70] Ibid, 6-7.

depository of truths beyond human discovery, momentous, practical, maintained one and the same in substance in every age from its first, and addressed to all mankind. And it has actually been embraced and is found in all parts of the world, in all climates, among all races, in all ranks of society, under every degree of civilization, from barbarism to the highest cultivation of mind."[71]

The human problems of huge and frightening proportions spawned by the changes we witness today, are already familiar. What may seem rather more exciting is the wide-ranging rapport among cultures these sudden changes have generated: they have fashioned a cross-cultural life-force, a cross-pollination of civilizations stemming from the beautiful motley of cultures springing from various parts of the world. These rapid and monumental changes which characterize our times have had remarkable consequences not only on Christian mission but also on wide-reaching universal concerns. Where previously social institutions were steady and stable, in our day things are floppy and fluctuating. Interreligious dialogue and church ecumenism, for some time now, have become battlegrounds in the Church. Consequent upon this, debates over the post-Second Vatican Council's place as a symbol of inclusive Catholicism have yet to be settled, yet the Church is already being thrown another challenge – this time, over Interculturalism. This cross-cultural phenomenon has invaded especially urban and city centers, and today, it has left the tiptoeing stage and is conquering the countryside and the developing regions of the globe. Tantalizing as this may be, in yielding that we are invaded today by such cultural forces, it does not make the leap of faith that is required to state the obvious: that John Henry Newman has, in sometime past, attempted these global matters with poise, proficiency and pride. Over the course of his life, he showed his teeth in the cause of truth and the education of the mind. His treatises in the university would not simply address the university challenges, but also the application of ethical and theological values and the imbibing of life principles gained through the study of various world cultural currents.

---

[71] J. H. NEWMAN, *An Essay in aid of a Grammar of Assent*, (London: Longmans Green and Co, 1902), 430-431.

Newman most especially believed in global mindfulness – what he baptized the *imperial mind*. He was thus of the conviction that culture (in the way he saw knowledge) was susceptible to change; that it was provisional, challengeable and developed over time. He was of the same conviction with John Paul II that 'a faith that does not become culture is a faith not fully accepted, not entirely thought out, not faithfully lived'[72]; for in his own words,

> The religious life of a people is of a certain quality and direction, and these are tested by the mode in which it encounters the various opinions, customs and institutions which are submitted to it. Drive a stake(stick) into a river's bed, and you will at once ascertain which way it is running, and will see which way the wind blows; submit your heretical and Catholic principle to the action of the multitude, and you will be able to pronounce at once whether it is imbued with Catholic truth or with heretical falsehood.[73]

Evidently, it is impossible to overstate John Henry Newman's influence on inculturation, that is, the literary, the philosophical, the historical and the theological education of man. Others are better qualified to talk about the first two, but as he announces his (gentle and measured) entry into the family of doctors of the Church, I offer a thought about him on the historical and theological education, which, is that, contemporary Christian theology and history have conceivably been a commentary on the theological opinions of this intellectual colossus. Undeniably language is central to the foundation of society. Keenly aware of the sheer influence of human language to human community, Newman fortified his English people to a theological principle very dear to language and education:

---

[72] JOHN PAUL II, *Address to the Italian National Congress of the Ecclesial Movement for Cultural Commitment*, (1982), 2.
[73] J. H. NEWMAN, *On Consulting the Faithful in Matters of Doctrine*, (Oxford: A Sheed & Ward Book, 2006), 75.

…if we do not use the vernacular; I do not see how the bulk of the Catholic people are to be catechized or taught at all. English has innovated on the Latin sense of its own Latin words; and if we are to speak according to the conditions of the language, and are to make ourselves intelligible to the multitude, we shall necessarily run the risk of startling those who are resolved to act as mere critics and scholastics in the process of popular instruction." This divergence from a classical or ecclesiastical standard is a great inconvenience, I grant; but we cannot remodel our mother-tongue. *Crimen* does not properly mean *crime*; *amiable* does not yet convey the idea of *amabilis*; *compassio* is not *compassion*; *princeps* is not a *prince*; *disputatio* is not *a dispute*; *praevenire* is not *to prevent*; *Cicero imperator* is not *the Emperor Cicero*; *scriptor egregius* is not *an egregious writer*; *virgo singularis* is not *a singular virgin*; *retractare dicta* is not *to retract what he has said*; and as we know from the sacred passage, *traducere* is not necessarily *to traduce*.[74]

Newman's genius for the vernacular would today seem to restate the significance of inculturation in the Christian theological landscape. Because we are finite beings, we have only a limited knowledge of our own and others' culture. Yet, God has endowed us with the capacity to learn and grow. This dynamism of man is the precondition for deepening his understanding of the way of life, of the culture of the other. By examining Newman in the light of intercultural pedagogy vis-à-vis current concerns we are delving into the province of whether he remains relevant to the twenty-first-century's age of globalization. What I am saying is that the radicalism of Newman's theological thought (engrossed in culture and conscience), was ahead of its time. Nothing is satisfactorily understood except in its connection to other happenings, to other cultures. For the most acceptable understanding, depiction, and illumination of a people we must

---

[74] *Ibid.*, 56-57.

look to their culture, which means the acquired spectacles through which they see life. His *On Consulting the Faithful in Matters of Doctrine* and *The Development of Christian Doctrine* are the measured masterpieces he particularly weaved to highlight the place of culture and experience in Christian thought. Newman in *On Consulting* for instance, demonstrates how theologians should go along it especially when relating to the Magisterium:

> This is not however, to advocate for licentiousness: it must be liberty under law. The liberty to make mistakes must be accompanied by the obligation to receive reproof when in error... our privilege is to speak out, but Rome's duty is to speak back – equally warmly and equally definitely since warmth and definiteness are required from both sides.[75]

And what is inculturation? It is the mastery of the meanings, the purposes and the fascinations of one's local social order. It is the formation of my mind and heart to loving my people, our values, our state of life and to bringing such values to bear on external powerful currents and influences that are dear to my heart. Inculturation is self-knowledge in the collective sense; for:

> Without self-knowledge you have no root in yourselves personally; you may endure for a time, but under affliction or persecution your faith will not last. This is why many in this age (and in every age) become infidels, heretics, schismatics, disloyal despisers of the Church. They cast off the form of truth, because it never has been to them more than a form. They endure not, because they never have tasted that the Lord is gracious; and they never have

---

[75] *Ibid.*, 35.

had experience of His power and love, because they have never known their own weakness and need.[76]

While we acknowledged that truth is full and whole and therefore found in God, we can no longer escape the reliable conviction that the most illuminating appreciation of truth comes via concrete real life and incarnated experience. Culture is that incarnated reality which Jesus sanctioned when he took human flesh. The human flesh of our cultures is worth the attention of the theologian today – what Newman saw as 'historical consciousness'. No doubt Lash underlines that "Newman was one of the first catholic theologians seriously to attempt to hold in tension the demands of historical consciousness and the Christian conviction that the gospel of Jesus Christ is irreplaceable and unchangeable."[77] But Newman's vision of culture or knowledge or experience was continuous enlargement of the spheres. Culture was culture when it opened its mental faculties to values from other cultures –what he named *the enlargement of the mind*. It would be a pleasure to know what spot John Henry Newman sat when he wrote the words 'enlargement of the mind'. Among all Newman's phrases, his 'enlargement of the mind' conveys the biggest percentage of interculture, taking the largest room in the human mind, and conquering absolute ground in the human heart. It is therefore possible to appreciate the full import of his contribution to intercultural pedagogy through the symbols he paints in, for example, the *Idea of a University*. In this emblematic effort he underlines the complexity and interrelation of true knowledge. Knowledge becomes a metaphor for shared human flourishing: All over the place there is linkage, there is the piecing together, there is relation. The result is a cultural give-and-take, that is, a cross-cultural illumination of persons – what Newman himself calls the enlargement of the mind.

The deferential, almost fascinating spell his words hold is by no means flamboyant or merely customary as a casual reader might

---

[76] J. H. NEWMAN, *Parochial and Plain Sermons*, Vol. I, (London: Longmans, Green, and Co., 1907), 55.

[77] NICHOLAS LASH, *Newman and Development: The Search for an Explanation in History,* (New York: Sheed & Ward 1975), 2.

think. Perhaps the best way to understand our indebtedness to him in intercultural education is to encapsulate his contribution into the following piquant words about enlarging the cultural mind:

> The enlargement consists, not merely in the passive reception into the mind of a number of ideas unknown to it, but in the mind's energetic and simultaneous action upon and towards and among those new ideas, which are rushing in upon it. It is the action of a formative power, reducing to order and meaning the matter of our acquirements; …We feel our minds to be growing and expanding then, when we not only learn, but refer what we learn to what we know already. It is not the mere addition to our knowledge that is the illumination; but the locomotion, the movement onwards, of that mental centre, to which both what we know, and what we are learning, the accumulating mass of our acquirements, gravitates. And therefore a truly great intellect, and recognized to be such by the common opinion of mankind, such as the intellect of Aristotle, or of St. Thomas, or of Newton, or of Goethe, (I purposely take instances within and without the Catholic pale, when I would speak of the intellect as such,) is one which takes a connected view of old and new, past and present, far and near, and which has an insight into the influence of all these one on another; without which there is no whole, and no centre. It possesses the knowledge, not only of things, but also of their mutual and true relations; knowledge, not merely considered as acquirement, but as philosophy.[78]

Interculturality, - that is, the mutual relation of ways of life, - is the multifaceted yet accomplished wisdom of a community, the tidy and ripe improvement of mind, the broadening or development of

---

[78] J. H. NEWMAN, *The Idea of a University*, 134.

awareness, a sagacious and all-inclusive outlook of other cultures; in fact, the science, philosophy and religion of a people. Intercultural activity consists not merely in the lifeless welcoming into the mind of a number of notions previously foreign to the mind; it is a robust and symphonic stroke of all the muscles of the mind and heart, of all the powers of dialogue and human encounter – it is the chic concurrence and lively confluence of more world views, more cultures, more mental landscapes. Hear Newman again – this time on history:

> Again, the study of history is said to enlarge and enlighten the mind, and why? because, as I conceive, it gives it a power of judging of passing events, and of all events, and a conscious superiority over them, which before it did not possess. And in like manner, what is called seeing the world, entering into active life, going into society, travelling, gaining acquaintance with the various classes of the community, coming into contact with the principles and modes of thought of various parties, interests, and races, their views, aims, habits and manners, their religious creeds and forms of worship,—gaining experience how various yet how alike men are, how low-minded, how bad, how opposed, yet how confident in their opinions; all this exerts a perceptible influence upon the mind, which it is impossible to mistake, be it good or be it bad, and is popularly called its enlargement.[79]

Interculturalism gives us a power of judging passing events and claims an authority over them which is able to judge history not on the side of power but on the side of truth, not on the side of imperial bigotry, but on the side of clearheaded wisdom. Newman speaks to the bargain, even of the enlargement of our religious perspective:

> On the other hand, Religion has its own enlargement, and an enlargement, not of tumult, but of peace. It

---

[79] *Ibid.*, 132.

is often remarked of uneducated persons, who have hitherto thought little of the unseen world, that, on their turning to God, looking into themselves, regulating their hearts, reforming their conduct, and meditating on death and judgment, heaven and hell, they seem to become, in point of intellect, different beings from what they were.[80]

It is hence no exaggeration to say that religious enlargement leads man to peace - peace in our hearts, peace in our homes. No one can deny the splendor and magnificence cultures have wrought on the effulgence of the human family and of true religion. It would then be a bending of the true definition to say that culture is a special category of activity, making it look like only the learned and gurus are 'cultured' - where the run of nameless masses who humbly do culture and need no one to blow their trumpet are discarded like so much humbug. So Newman was also the child of his age, as he makes difficult distinctions between cultures: "…and thus the civilization of modern times remains what it was of old, not Chinese, or Hindoo, or Mexican or Saracenic, or of any new description hitherto unknown, but the lineal descendant, or rather the continuation, *mutatis mutandis*, of the civilization which began in Palestine and Greece." [81] But culture – as we shall see – carries meaning beyond what his age offered. The 18th century's smug depiction of "culture" as something greater than what the regular run of people do, is to me, one of the signs of that century's inventive flaw. Culture – authentic culture - is the common accord of a people, the practice and customs of the people which practice and customs are held as law. These things are jewels to evangelization. And anywhere these jewels are cast-off for whatever evangelical high-sounding reason, the Gospel agonizes.

The *Cor ad cor loquitur* of Cardinal Newman not simply did symbolize his remarkable faith experience, but also highlighted one of the pedagogic principles dear to his heart - personal influence. To Newman, "It requires one to be intimate with a person, to have a chance

---

[80] *Ibid.,* 133.
[81] J. H. NEWMAN, *The Idea of a University*, 253.

of doing him good"[82]. You experience this when you travel. You have all kinds of ideas in the mind about what people from other climes and countries are like. How they are diverse and sometimes strange. Thus the name stranger or visitor. Such remoteness to the other person creates a theoretical idea, a sweeping impression, and thus engenders stereotypes about them. Once as rector of the Irish Catholic university Newman was absent from school and there arose a disciplinary problem that needed his attention. He informed Ornsby on his standpoint about the matter in the following words: 'I have ever acted, not by formal authority and rule, but by influence, and this power cannot be well exerted when absent'.[83] The knowledge of the concrete individual, this power of the concrete, Newman had once called it in another great work, "real assent."[84] In the example of Newman, I recount a personal experience I witnessed the first month I arrived in Europe.

That was six years ago, precisely in October 2012 when I arrived Rome for post-graduate studies. About three weeks after my arrival, I was invited one evening for a birthday party of one of our European colleagues in the Pontifical Irish College, our residence. An African friend – who had lived in that residence before – strongly advised me to take money along. I didn't see the need since I was invited. I reluctantly picked some coins as we took off to the restaurant, for the birthday meal. "You're enjoying it," the host passed around and threw these words. We were served our orders and the party meal went along. As the meal was getting to its close, almost everyone went for their wallets while I watched with interest as they busied to get the amount they are to each pay. "Gerald please can't you see it's time for payment…I told you," came the words of my African pal. Feeling really dumbfounded and upset, I uttered a desperate: "I can't believe this!" I then went for my wallet to ferret the lone coins that I threw in. As luck would have it, it reached the amount needed. I handed it to my country's colleague whispering in utter disbelief, "Is this true?"

That was the celebration of birthday in Italy, I thought, – so strange.

---

[82] J. H. NEWMAN, *Letters and Diaries*, to his sister Jemima (8 February 1829).
[83] J. H. NEWMAN, *Letters and Diaries*, Newman to Ornsby, (31 December 1857)
[84] See his work *An Essay in Aid of Grammar of Assent*.

I intend to draw from these somewhat insignificant birthday meeting, pretty weighty conclusions which at first glance might seem fairly out of proportion; but only, I hope, at first glance. The me, perhaps partly because of my fresh beginnings in Italy, but I believe also for much deeper and more critical reasons, is evidently ignorant that the culture of my Nso (Cameroonian people), is merely one out of a million other cultures of the world and full of illogicalities and unusual customs, like every other culture, imagines that I need to wage cultural war against the birthday host, for asking too much of me. The other person (my host) being fully aware that I just arrived their country could not be excused on the grounds of his culture. Lack of knowledge might be a more likely reason; but here again I believe that something more intentional than mere ignorance was at work. Could it not be already this tendency that my host's way of life is the universal norm and therefore any of us around should toe the line of the civilized culture?

Definitely, at issue here is a clash of cultural outlooks. In my culture, if one offers to take you for a meal, it is understood that the one extending the invitation is footing the bill. Besides, I just arrived Rome and I thought at least I should be considered a guest among colleagues who were not only better-off but had been in the college before. That is what African Ubuntu cultural exigencies implore its members – be they in Cameroon, Kenya or South Africa. But I had to learn from that day that I was already in new strange grounds. The cultural shock was overwhelming – but fathomable.

I suppose an honest tête-à-tête with my host could have been helpful for all of us. In the recent literature on the human social condition, there is an emerging consensus dismissal of what might be considered cultural diversity. This essay offers an argument for such intercultural encounter. This debate is projected to shift attention from intolerant social populism that is dominating political discourse today and to open-mindedly expect these cultural consequences thus enabling an enlargement of cultural perspectives. This practice is not new; which should relieve us all of substantial blame and possibly make us even willing to face this phenomenon objectively. This is the tip of the iceberg of the prominence of intercultural pedagogy today.

A lot of us have spent some time telling our children or trainees some fairly challenging stuff. That to be successful in life they must go beyond their comfort zones. That what is good for the goose is good for the gander. That they are equal in dignity to all human beings. That their minds should be enlarged in such a way as to welcome diverse and challenging views. That there is no end to the pursuit of facts about other cultures. That love is noble and contagious and should be enabled. These simple little things are weighty cultural values that have emotional impact on people. You don't even need to go that far to what is wrong with not teaching children these simple lessons of life. And therefore we can never overemphasize the importance of exchange of cultural values among societies, among countries and among continents. The truth about the world is not in one person, one culture, one custom, one history. The truth about things is in men and women, in cultures, in customs, and in all histories. And if you wish to get the real truth about something as Newman says: "In order to have possession of the truth at all, we must have the whole truth; and no one science, no two sciences, no one family of sciences, nay, not even all secular science, is the whole truth.". John Henry Newman never used the word *globalization* – but if he was alive today I am not surprised he would. Had he ever had the occasion to remark on it, he would have looked at it from the Catholic point of view, as the word actualizing his ecclesial conviction of oneness, of a totalizing universalism best applied in the idea of the Catholicism he professed with all his might, at the second phase of his life.

Of course, there are those who would strive to persuade you that, since Newman spoke enormously about Western civilization, what he proposed for us today is the conquest of the Western Mind, and therefore the slaying of other civilizations as some have thought; and they will quote the venerable Pope Benedict XVI to sustain a theory, which would lead to utter insipidity. I say that there was no place for triteness in John Henry Newman. Newman saw the beauty of Greek/Italian cultures (European civilization) and valorized them. But Newman did not fail to applaud the Mexican cultures (the civilization of the Americas), the Egyptian/Saracenic cultures(African civilization), the Chinese/Hindu cultures (Asian civilization):

> Looking then at the countries which surround the Mediterranean Sea as a whole, I see them to be, from time immemorial, the seat of an association of intellect and mind, such as to deserve to be called the Intellect and the Mind, of the Human Kind. Starting as it does and advancing from certain centres, till their respective influences intersect and conflict, and then at length intermingle and combine, a common Thought has been generated, and a common Civilization defined and established. Egypt is one such starting point Syria another, Greece a third, Italy a fourth, and North Africa a fifth, - afterwards France and Spain.[85]

Christianity came into being within a variegated cultural background. One particular intermingling of cultures witnessed was that of the ancient Jewish and the Greek cultural worldviews. The Christian formation seeks to bring its truths in new and inventive ways, and such is done through the apparatus of the new cultural settings in what is currently called inculturation.

Then came Emperor Constantine, who was happily baptized to Christianity. His 312 conversion was thrilling news to the Church, but later, this news wrought in grieve to global Church mission. The mono-cultural missionary narrative that accompanied his entry into Christendom began annexing the world. With political power to modify missionary activity, Constantine's "Christianity took on a single cultural form that shaped its forms of worship and its theological categories for more than a thousand years. Cultural diversity, associated as it was with new ways of living and reflecting on the faith, were often actively resisted." [86] This mono-cultural pastoral parochialism would swell the size of baptized fold but would reduce ecclesial quality in the damage it would cause some mankind's peoples and their cultures.

---

[85] J. H. NEWMAN, *The Idea of a University*, 252.
[86] W. A. DYRNESS, "Crosscultural Theology", in W. A. Dyrness – V. Karkkainen, in *Global Dictionary of Theology*, (2008), 214.

Some similar thing would come up in the 16th, 17th, 18th and 19th centuries in the celebrated radiance of the industrial revolution and of the Enlightenment. And we must begin that Technology and Enlightenment were salutary happenings in the history of humanity. But the bigoted mono-cultural claims of its forerunners would overrun even the evangelizing mission of the Church institution they detested so ferociously. During this period "the universal project of Christendom was replaced by a belief in a universal reason that was seen as the key to unlocking the secrets of history and nature."[87] The blinkered view that one culture was the only culture and therefore civilization, took over again as "many of the enlightenment writers reveal an assumption that reason has access to a harmonious reality, the knowledge of which would lead humankind into a glorious future. Writers in the later twentieth century have shown the way this universalizing tendency led to many of the disasters of that war-torn century."[88] The Christian had been cuckolded into this seemingly plausible but perilous cultural universalism:

> Christians of the eighteenth-century missionary movements were deeply influenced by Enlightenment ideas and understood Western civilization and learning as the privileged form in which the gospel should be expressed. As Christianity was the supreme truth of religion, so Western civilization was setting the standard to which all other cultures should aspire. So closely was Christianity associated with the abstract truth of the Enlightenment that diversity of interpretation, and indeed cultural diversity more generally, were treated as enemies.[89]

The menacing phenomenon saw its full-blown perils in Africa. It would carry the world into the worst crime man has ever committed to man: the transatlantic slave trade. Since he saw himself as the acme

---

[87] *Ibid.*
[88] *Ibid.*
[89] *Ibid.*

of humanity and his culture as world civilization, he could treat the 'African bushman' as nothing and his land as the 'dark continent'. Society had witnessed enough of this savagery. The self-styled *mission civilatrice* would take a foul full-scale feat in Napoleon Bonaparte's 1798 invasion of Egypt with a horde of researchers, historians, writers and excavators with clear orders to take (or better still pillage) Egypt's antique treasures to France.[90] These were really regretful moments for African cultures.

In the Twentieth century the wheel of history turned full circle. Indigenous cultures would begin to enthrone themselves "as a result of the rise of anthropological studies ethnic diversity came to be appreciated, whether critically or uncritically." [91] - and thus the overhauling of cross-cultural thinking and theology. Today, thanks to these changes, an African kingdom stands out proudly with its culture. Its people see God through the spectacles of their culture and sees God more beautifully as such.

This creative intercourse between Christianity and Cultures – which gives rise to inculturation - was Newmanian. He was of the strong conviction that theology was best explained in the lingua franca of a community, if by theology we (as he understood) mean easing the understanding of faith for God's people. And the Latin (or Italian) pages that Vatican pronouncements carry should be simplified into simple English for the English local faithful. The way of life, that is, the culture of the people(the laity) is imperative, and Newman is one with St. Augustine of Hippo:

> Furthermore, the common accord of the faithful, of populations and of nations, is – as St Augustine points out – one of the chief factors which holds us, justly, within the bosom of the Church, and 'in matters whereupon the Scripture has not spoken clearly, the

---

[90] See T. HUNT, "Once Britain's culture wielded global power. Now France shows us the way", in *The Guardian*, 5-11-2017, https://www.theguardian.com/commentisfree/2017/nov/05/one-britains-culture-wielded-global-power-now-france-shows-way.

[91] *Ibid.*

custom of the people of God, or the institutions of our predecessors, are to be held as law'.[92]

The 'common accord of the faithful, of the populations, and of the nations' mentioned above, is essentially the inculturated faith of the people, what is famously called *consensus fidelium*. The subject of Newman's *On Consulting* is in essence, the theme of inculturation of faith in England. And thus when he says for example that "for myself, I am accustomed to lay great stress on the *consensus fidelium*" he certifies that inculturation is the lifeblood of his theology; and that experience, history and culture are highly regarded words in the theological enterprise. The struggles with the Arian heresy (which he tellingly illustrates in his *On Consulting*) was certainly the struggle of cultures outside the mainline Empire for intercourse with the Gospel. It was an early Church's tussle to inculturate the faith - the tension between the Word of God and the cultural currents existing in the surroundings. The result of such struggle was inculturation of faith manifest in the pronouncements of the various local and ecumenical councils of the time. And therefore Athanasius, Hilary, Basil, Gregory Nazianzen, Ambrose, Jerome, Augustine, the monks of Egypt, Origen are pioneering icons of Christian theological inculturation.

Permeating world discourse today is the sense that humanity has wandered away from God's path. I argue that one of the problems with treating immigrants like mere things in some countries today is that selfishness has prevented us from seeing what's wonderful about empathy and humanity. And with what I see coming, only a virile confrontation with history and forthright trading of ideas coupled with a clear-eyed look at cultures can help us forge a new path forward. Perhaps, the real tour of discovery today consists not in seeing new lands but in seeing overlooked values. An understanding of the cultures of other people today is an understanding of our global selves, an understanding that the world is our home. And therefore fostering cultural exchange is the way to best prepare the up-and-

---

[92] J. H. NEWMAN, *On Consulting the Faithful in Matters of Doctrine*, (Oxford: A Sheed & Ward Book, 2006), 22-23.

coming generation. It is in this framework that "the worldwide network of ecclesiastical universities and faculties is called to offer the decisive contribution of leaven, salt and light of the Gospel of Jesus Christ and the living Tradition of the Church, which is ever open to new situations and ideas."[93] Education of the mind and heart can do much to bring change. But if it cannot immediately answer the pressing issues at stake, still there is need to delve, pedagogically, into the problem and therefrom propose a new academic policy that can smoothen the helpful interaction of diverse political, social and anthropological systems invading world cities today. Consequently, to Newman, the true Christian believer, the true Christian thinker, the true Christian theologian is the cross-cultural Christian - the one who is firmly rooted in his native culture and his Christianity, and whose soul is so enlarged to embrace other schools of thought, other cultures, other customs, other peoples. This is because:

> No good could come of merely imitating the Fathers for imitating sake; rather, such servility is likely to prevent the age from developing Church principles so freely as it might otherwise do. Even the Fathers were of different Schools. The respective characters of the Alexandrian, Antiochene, Roman and African are distinctively marked. Again it is hardly possible to deny that Augustine's theology is in a certain sense what may be called a second edition of the Catholic Tradition, the transmission of the primitive stream through an acute, rich, and powerful mind. Another change took place in point of tone and view…in the theology o the Schoolmen. And there have been other great changes since, involving changes in the moral state and (what may be called) *mind* of the Church, and that over and above the silent progress which society has been making, the revolutions of civil government, the march of civilization and, what

---

[93] FRANCIS, APOSTOLIC CONSTITUTION *Veritatis Gaudium* on ecclesiastical Universities and Faculties, 29-I-2018, 3.

has necessarily attended upon it, a far more active and excited state of the public mind. These causes must have produced and must be still producing their several effects, greater or less, upon us, such as would extend at last to our theology. Indeed we cannot suppose any set of events of this nature to leave the world exactly where they found it; they would influence, or alarm, or develop, or direct the minds of divines, as the case might be.[94] (Ess. 1, 287-88)

Since each and every human is made in the image and likeness of God, though we are each diverse and unique, we are as expected, interactive creatures. God is Himself Love and he passes his laws through communication. Revealed truth comes to us through relation, – Jesus Christ meeting mankind. So interculture is established in the office of the human heart through God's own interaction with us. The body of Christ the Church exhorts us to communicate the Gospel to all nations. Even though we are in God's image, we are limited beings. Therefore our lives are dependent on the lives of others. This interdependence is the reality of diversity impacting on us which accrues from the need to dialogue and to love. The law of love of neighbor is therefore at the center of intercultural theology, since Jesus says "I am the way …." (Jn 14:6). He has opened this way to many ways which all lead to him. There is beauty in diversity, he knows – the diversity that allows for a particular Way that leads to God. "love one another as I have loved you…" (John 14:6). Both these arguments of Christ must lead us in our exploration as we strive to probe into intercultural communication, the standing of other cultural life-ways in the collective framework of global communion. In each of these areas the theology of the kingdom of God is public theology, which therefore participates in the *res publica* of society and engages itself in critical and prophetic terms because it sees the public reality in the light of the coming reign of God.

---

[94] J. H. NEWMAN, *Essays: Critical and Historical*, Vol. 2, (London: Aeterna Press, 1871), 201.

Rootedness in culture empowers rootedness in the Gospels, for genuine missionary work aims at all times to purify the rudimentary features of homegrown cultures, without counterfeiting or faking them. A culturally disenfranchised Christian is a vacillating Christian. When Jesus prompts us that he is the Way, we all with Thomas join in, agreeing, unreservedly, "my Lord and my God". Christianity is from the very beginning a Way. Ways are born only if people run through them. They disappear when not used. The Way of Christ strikes root in peoples' hearts. In those hearts, the Way generates many ways. These generated ways are fashioned when Christianity comes into contact with cultures. Because of its rapport with cultures, the Way takes the form of ways as it encounters human hearts, diverse ways that at the last day would come back to the Way, the Truth and the Life. Because it is the Way, two convictions must sink ever deeper about the power given at Pentecost: how the Early Church evolved from an ethnic community in Jerusalem to an intercultural congregation in Antioch. And how the Holy Spirit generated the Church to a stronghold of unity that respects human cultures, esteems diverse ways of life not in a uniformity but in a cross-cultural concord. Pentecost marks a turning point in the life of the people of God – there is a Jew, there is a Gentile. God's Spirit has made it possible for everyone to spread the word in his native tongue in their historical, cultural ways, and be heard by other people of other cultures. Pentecost Day becomes a moment time to ponder over the often-ignored pastoral art of inculturation and Interculturality.

Luke tells us in that great work of the Acts that people from all over the world upheld their tongues (cultures) and heard "in their own tongue the mighty works of God". If there is a lesson to learn from these beginnings of the Church it is this, that diversity of expression is at the heart of making Church? In fact, the gift of the Pentecost is more the gift of 'ears', of not only speaking but also listening and understanding the other. The Pentecost Day preserved cultures but also allowed the human spirit freedom to receive the whisperings of God in other tongues.

Hospitality is best practiced when offering food and drink, for culture is very well fashioned by the drudgery and rituals surrounding its food. The table therefore is foremost to the study of intercultural pedagogy – both at home and the Church. The theme of banqueting, of meal and drink is central to the ministry of Jesus and to intercultural education. "When you give a luncheon or a dinner, do not invite your friends or your brothers or you relatives or rich neighbors, in case they may invite you in return, and you would be repaid. But when you give a banquet, invite the poor, the crippled, the lame, the blind. And you will be blessed, because they cannot repay you." (Luke 14: 12-14) This is of course the prelude to the Parable of the Banquet, but it already suggests Christ's sensibility to the dignity of the other people - especially the dignity of those who cannot pay you back. It is a powerful metaphor of the respect of each person's way of life and it is a way of showing that culture is not culture because I am rich or 'refined'. Culture is culture because there are people – which ever type of people.

The biblical story of Jesus and the Samaritan woman serves as an archetype for intercultural pedagogy. One sunny afternoon in Samaria, two incompatible people meet beside a well. They are all from two estranged cultural worlds. One is a woman whose name is not identified. Another is a man whose name is Jesus. The brief conversation was a life-changer for the weaker person – and is a brilliant picture of unadulterated cross-cultural encounter.

There are many lessons here about this encounter. But I like to identify two: racial prejudice and intercultural dialogue. But more so it teaches us who to evangelize in an intercultural diverse world. This encounter is more significant in content in that it is the longest conversation Jesus ever had with someone – not even with his disciples. As Jesus engages the Samaritan woman into conversation, her biases are instantly aroused. They are summed up in this ethnocentric and prejudiced statement: "you, a Jew, ask a drink of me, a woman of Samaria", (John 4:9). This racial prejudice was deeply rooted in the interactions among Jews and Samaritans: "you are an outsider". All this dates back to a very long history of rivalry. The woman is fixated on Jesus' Jewishness and her preconceptions, but Jesus stage-manages to elevate the tête-à-tête toward spiritual certainties. The woman's vision is blurred by the conditions of her personal story and background. The mask of racism and intolerance is gradually hauled up the woman's tribal petty perspective. Jesus accomplishes this by a courteous and compassionate interchange within the lady's specific conditions and comforts, for instance, Jacob's well, marital record, and worshipping in Gerizim versus Jerusalem. As the archetype of cross-cultural encounter, Jesus is conscious of social dissimilarities, well-informed of the woman's cares, clever in his method, and sympathetically ready to satisfy her needs. This encounter of Jesus with the Samaritan woman not only explains why the Church has from the beginning regarded encounter with all human cultures as an inviolable requirement for evangelizing missionary territories; it also shows us how intimately the Holy Spirit is linked to the Church of Christ.

The nascent Christian community in Jerusalem affords us an opportunity to rediscover how the Holy Spirit willed that intercultural encounter would be the Church's Way. And thus, the Pentecost Experience is the most defining moment for the Church. It is significant not only for our individual spiritual benefit but most especially for the collective experience of an intercultural character. And thus, intercultural pedagogy is against tendencies that propagate inequalities among humans. So its good news challenges head-on deeply implanted colonial convictions and patronizing attitudes. To this temperament and using the words of the famous Canadian anthropologist, intercultural pedagogy warns the colonizing intimidator or empire diehard: "The world in which you were born is just one model of reality. Other cultures are not failed attempts at being you; they are unique manifestations of the human spirit."[95] Interculturalism is the key anchor of all serious knowledge today. It is the arbitrator between people and people, between nature and grace, between culture and dogma, between kingdoms and states, between nations and continents, between the human race and God. It is ancillary to the overwhelming power of the Holy Spirit in the world. It ministers not only to world bodies like the UNO but also to religious bodies like Catholicism.

---

[95] WADE DAVIS, *The Wayfinders: Why Ancient Wisdom Matters in the Modern World*, (Toronto: House of Anansi, 2009).

Christianity embraces globalization, but the globalization which is harmless to peoples' cultures, one which is a communion of many cultures respected in their various diversities, one which collectively converses and shares riches. Consequently, the Pentecost intercultural experience is not the Babel of globalization today which claims to speak one unbroken language. Rather, the Holy Spirit of Pentecost confers each culture the right to deferentially express self in its own language and to be understood by others in that language. The Christ-event bids the people of all nations to open up and embrace the great contributions of other philosophies and cultures and know that life is not a one-point-of-view enterprise. This exchange of ideas, this attention to the other, the capacity to fathom the other, and also to transform oneself is what intercultural pedagogy proliferates.

It is true that Babel is metaphor of the confusion of languages and therefore has come to mean a condemnation of human pride, a vain pride that aims to build a tall tower in competition with the omnipotent God. But, indeed, this pluralism, this confusion of tongues, is a return to the aboriginal intention of God to bring together not only the union between man and woman, but also to acknowledge the multiplicity and encounter of races. Christianity therefore conveys a universal. The universal it expresses is not patronizing power. It is the warning sign that we are custodians of Mother Earth; and that the God who is father of both Gentile and Jew, is calling the human family. The aim of such studies is to bring careful attention to bear on the question of the dignity of despised immigrants, the dignity of other people's way of life, and the liberation of enslaved peoples from colonial strongholds. What we like to emphasize here is that though there is a pedagogy, that is, though there is a theory (and which theory is so indispensable), theology of interculture is a praxis. It is concrete pragmatic theology.

So what in all this distinguishes Intercultural Pedagogy today? If I have a point to drive home, it is that, it is the discovery of man's resource, – the recognition of empathy in man's soul; that is, it is the unearthing of human sensitivity, and the perception of values even when still within the human heart. Intercultural pedagogy argues the case for the social, moral and spiritual benefits of cultural exchange, while also exploring the disadvantage of collective division. It is a mission of hope injected in the social fabric and calling on the academic milieu to encounter and confront with new interdisciplinary approaches, eternal themes like justice in the world, the human thirst for freedom, a revisiting of the ancient message of love of the stranger, preservation of human dignity and a transition from mere multicultural cohabitation to the building of an intercultural reality articulated in dialogue, negotiation and peace. What a cook is in culinary science, such is intercultural pedagogy in the province of theology today. The authentic cook originates meals from the application of varied ingredients, diverse cooking techniques – fashioning a meal out of his urbane inventive pool. Such a meal – like Interculturality – is garlanded with hospitality, warmth, fellow feeling, openheartedness, and convivial conversation. A theology lacking these soul-stirring and revitalizing values these days, is deceased theology.

Cultural intercourse today has a history, as we're reminded when we explore the fundamentals of the intercultural phenomenon. What we recognize as genuine globalization has profound roots in the Biblical story. Adam and Eve saw the vast Garden of Eden as a simple containable village tied to the center by the love of their creator God. During their stay with plants and animals and the seas, there was responsible traffic across that early world. This traffic continues today among cultures and the gospels as thinkers like Newman have made us know. Indeed, If the mark of a great thinker is that he connects the worlds, then John Henry Newman is really a great man, for his literary yield has succeeded to connect knowledge to knowledge, civilizations to civilizations and ancient times to our times.

Intercultural pedagogy unlocks the huge, untapped potential of our diverse, multicultural society; and muddles the strong dismal tidal waves that seek to divide mankind. There can be no question about it: Newman's work exist near the edge where the ungoverned waters of critical thought meet the grave sphere of dogmatic standards. In so doing his intellectual harvest commands the Christian unaffected mind, posing a promise that is realized but unfulfilled, difficult to envisage yet practicable. He saw so well that "The Church fears no knowledge, but she purifies all, she represses no element of our nature, but cultivates the whole".[96] In fact, along with Augustine of Hippo and Thomas Aquinas, he has become today a god-like presence in Christian educational imagination as his pedagogic writings hold their supreme power beyond the page. And while it should be remembered that for now Cardinal Newman is going nowhere, that he has become one of the reigning champions of Christian scholarship, it is hard to avoid the feeling of satisfaction, of some seductively commonplace mood of composure within the human heart. The mission of the Church today is to keep lighting the flame of bliss and peace, to perennially awaken the nations to the knowledge of Transcendence, because the Church considers that her most essential and chief charge is to look beyond penultimate certainties and to seek those that are definitive. But the accomplishment of such a feat would not be apt if it is not begun from the known world of peoples' cultures and histories to the unknown world of grace and revealed truth. Hence, the disregard of the way of life or culture of a people is complete contempt not only of their way of life or culture, but it is the dehumanization of their own persons, for to strip them of culture is to rob them of dignity. It has happened in the past and our concern at present is that as cultures intermarry, no human community ever rob another human community of its culture, of its own way of life.

---

[96] J. H. NEWMAN, *The Idea of a University*, 234.

Chapter Six

SHADOWS INTO THE TRUTH

> And now, Gentlemen, I bring these remarks to a conclusion. What I would urge upon every one, whatever may be his particular line of research…is a great and firm belief in the sovereignty of Truth. Error may flourish for a time, but Truth will prevail in the end. The only effect of error ultimately is to promote Truth.
>
> *The Idea of a University*

Already from the title of Pope Francis' apostolic constitution on the university, *The Joy of the Truth (Veritatis Gaudium)*, it is evident the connection with John Henry Newman's all life passion, the truth. The event of the publication of *The Joy of the Truth* has signaled a new chapter in Church history and has opened an array of prospects and challenges for higher education. The apostolic constitution comes at a crucial time in the unfolding of world events which gives us the opportunity to debate the challenges facing the world. That Pope Francis chose the title of is remarkable documents on Higher Education *The Joy of Truth* is a mark not only of the high esteem he has for truth but also for his strong affiliations already to the spirit of John Henry Newman. In the journey of life the real champions are those who seek to propagate truth; those who seek to defend it and not wear it away or water it down. Newman sought to present always the truth in its raw aboriginal content. He searched for the truth mercilessly:

Truth can fight its own battle. It has a reality in it, which shivers to pieces swords of earth. As far as we are not on the side of truth, we shall shiver to bits, and I am willing it should be so....I see too that in the rising generation the most influential and stirring men in Church and State have in them a root of Catholic principles.[97]

Newman in *The Idea of a University* was clear about the workings and supremacy of truth. To him, if "the object of all sciences is truth", and persons employ reason in every branch of knowledge, "no matter what man he be, Hindoo, Mahometan, or infidel, his conclusions within his own science, according to the laws of that science, are unquestionable, and not to be suspected by Catholics, unless Catholics may legitimately be jealous of fact and truth, of divine principles and divine creations"[98] At the evening of his life he would advise in his will he be buried with the following epitaph on his tombstone: "Out of Shadows and Images into the Truth". Of course, everything that is true has according to John Henry Newman been always a "a root of Catholic principles" and that truth "has a power of its own, which makes its way". [99] His faith in the invincible power of truth was unshakeable.

Pope Francis has in recent times defiantly stood for the truth of the reality about suffering humanity in the poor immigrants and the oppressed and godforsaken peoples of the world. While Newman's prime focus is truth in ideas, Francis' prime occupation is the truth about our concrete reality, for to him: "Realities are greater than ideas."[100] The fact that God took human form, that he entered so intimately into our human reality marks the importance transcendence has for the reality about man and woman. The Word

---

[97] J. H. NEWMAN, *Grammar of Assent,* Longman Green and Co., London 1909, 92-93.
[98] J. H. NEWMAN, *The Idea of a University*, Longman Green and Co., London 1907.
[99] J. H. NEWMAN, *Fifteen Sermons Preached before the University Of Oxford*, Longman Green and Co., London 1909, 276.
[100] POPE FRANCIS, Apostolic Exhortation *Evangelii Gaudium*, 233.

made Flesh Jesus Christ sanctifies humanity with his own human reality and encourages us to evangelize that reality to the world. This is the novelty in the Second Vatican Council which puts human history in its rightful place. Man is not more ashamed of his history, man accepts his reality and seeks the help of God in giving that reality more and better meanings. Pope Francis views things from this point of direction. But all of them are of one mind about the inevitabilities about ideas and reality. In fact, to search for truth is the communication between ideas and reality, between mind and experience, between thought and concrete living. Would it not therefore be creditably true to say that these two (Francis and Newman) have been indomitable champions of the quest for truth? Without doubt, one thing that intellectually pulls these great men to each other is the fact – beautifully articulated by Newman - that truth is grounded in their cast-iron certainty in a compassionate God: "I have said that all branches of knowledge are connected together, because the subject-matter of knowledge is intimately united in itself, as being the acts and the work of the Creator."[101] Engaging in the issue about the companionship between Newman's pedagogy and the recent Popes' vision of Catholic higher education is a very rewarding responsibility.

Newman believed in the wisdom of the Church on scholarly matters. He did not only believe, he worked on them. A long history of Catholicism on the academic question is no concealed matter. The university has always been estimably regarded by the Church. In fact no chronicling of the beginnings of university studies can be complete without the explicit portrayal of the contribution of Christianity to its unfolding. There is a respected school of thought that holds strongly that the modern university indeed is a creation of the Church. Newman - a convinced Catholic and fully aware of who the Pope was and what the Pope championed in the world - dedicated himself completely to the service of the Dublin university when the Pope said the word. He entrusted his whole confidence

---

[101] J. H. NEWMAN, *The Idea of a University*, Longman Green and Co., London 1907, Discourse V, "Knowledge Its own End", 88.

in the decision of the Holy See and took up the rectorship of the university with the following endearing words:

> It is the decision of the Holy See; St. Peter has spoken, it is he who has enjoined that which seems to us so unpromising. He has spoken, and has a claim on us to trust him. He is no recluse, no solitary student, no dreamer about the past, no doter upon the dead and gone, no projector of the visionary …If ever there was a power on earth who had an eye for the times, who has confined himself to the practicable, and has been happy in his anticipations, whose words have been facts, and whose commands prophecies, such is he in the history of ages, who sits from generation to generation in the Chair of the Apostles, as the Vicar of Christ, and the Doctor of His Church.[102]

No doubt, we look at him today vis-à-vis the pontiffs of modern times, and it is refreshing to do so.

His connections with and knowledge of the issues of higher education for Catholics in Ireland would be the same and would comprise one of the keynote chapters of the book of his rich life. One of the reasons why Newman had problems with the proprietors of the Irish university – problems that later impaired the progress of the university and got Newman often thinking of resigning – was that the Irish Bishops never really were prepared for a full-blown university. They felt the need of something that was much similar to a seminary or a school that could compete with the colonial colleges that threatened Catholic indigenous Irish faith. You would see Newman unambiguously stating the facts to his onlookers influenced by the heat he was going through from his superiors: "If then a University is a direct preparation for this world, let it be what it professes. It is not a Convent, it is not a Seminary; it is a place to fit men of the world for the world." A university founded with the

---

[102] J. H. NEWMAN, *The Idea of a University*, Longman Green and Co., London 1907.

parochial ambition of serving only Irish concerns was – to Newman – no university at all. Newman saw his Irish University as serving the orbis terrarum, especially the world of Anglo-Saxon peoples all over the world. This background is important because it tells us why *The Idea of a University* is the lifeblood of his academic life.

Indeed, the very defining stamp of Newman's life is what a Newman scholar once called 'the very closeness of speech to speaker, of text to thinker'[103]. He made studies quite practical because he was always conscious of the pastoral bent of everything in his priestly life. Even in teaching, he wished not only to move the mind but also the heart of his learner. Paul Shrimpton the great Newman scholar and educationist shares the idea of this pastoral focus of Newman as he indicates to us that Newman did not share the recent narrow view of education many colleges and universities propagate today:

> As founding rector of the Catholic University, Newman did not sit in academic and administrative isolation, but acted as dean of one of the collegiate houses, located at 6 Harcourt Street. When the Archbishop of Dublin enquired from Rome about how the university was progressing, Newman responded not about its governance or student numbers but with a pastoral account of the house he was overseeing. This speaks volumes about his priorities.[104]

It is because of this pastoral instinct that Newman at one time avowed: 'An academical system without the personal influence of teachers upon pupils, is an arctic system; it will create an ice-bound, petrified, cast-iron University, and nothing else'[105] His life message was always that education was done when by doing it, it involves the

---

[103] NICHOLAS LASH, in "John Henry Newman: Teaching teachers", *Thinking Faith*, 3-8-2010.
[104] PAUL SHRIMPTON, in "Unthinkable: Has Cardinal John Henry Newman's vision for universities died?", *Irish Times*, 2-12-2014.
[105] J. H. NEWMAN, *Historical Sketches* iii. 74.

care of the soul of man too. Pope Francis in the Pontifical University at Chile reminded world Catholic institutes of higher learning that the evangelizing outreach and pastoral vitality are hallmarks of a true Catholic university today. The importance of broadening perspective, of widening not only our mental faculties but of bringing hearts to speak to hearts in a universal exchange of wisdom is what a powerhouse of knowledge like the university should inspire. This is what Pope Francis communicated to us through the rostrum of his Chilean university visit:

> I was pleased to learn of the evangelizing outreach and the joyful vitality of your university chaplaincy, which is a sign of a young, lively Church that "goes forth". The missions that take place each year in different parts of the country are an impressive and enriching reality. With these, you are able to broaden your outlook and encounter different situations that, along with regular events, keep you on the move. "Missionaries", in the etymological sense of the word, are never equal to the mission; they learn to be sensitive to God's pace through their encounter with all sorts of people who they either did not know, did not have daily contact with or were at a distance.[106]

Current Christian literature brings forward very frequently the name of Newman, and especially as his canonization looms the thing would take an exponential pace. In an age where technical and marketable education is exalted to the highest place, when every minute of college and university life is weighed in monetary terms, a work like Newman's *The Idea of a University* ought to be held in high esteem by all who still see education as the very exercise of promoting human flourishing;

---

[106] FRANCIS, Address at the Pontifical Catholic University, Santiago, Chile, Wednesday, 17 January 2018, https://www.vaticannews.va/en/pope/news/2018-01/chile-journey-visit-catholic-university.html.

I observe that the very same subjects of teaching, the Evidences of Christianity, the Classics, and much more Experimental Science, Modern History, and Biography, may be right in their proper place, as portions of one system of knowledge, suspicious, when detached or in had company...Not science only, not Literature only, not Theology only, either abstract knowledge whatever, is taken into account in a University, as being the special seat of that large Philosophy, which embraces and locates truth of every kind, and every method of attaining it.[107]

And this is how education was Newman's line - because he was concerned not only about the truth but the whole truth, and because he cared for standards but never neglected the person. He was occupied with the daunting task of preparing lectures, speeches and management but he never forgot that all that was meant to build up the human being, meant for human flourishing and never forgot he was a priest and pastor of souls.

In this Newmanian light and in the light of general university studies, the Argentinean Pope is of the conviction that true knowledge should not be knowledge-for-knowledge-sake. Knowledge should be exposed to the immediate community because knowledge is there for the society. In fact knowledge veiled in university buildings or in people's minds is not yet knowledge. This Pope Francis counsels that true Christian university knowledge should never be dissociated from the native and traditional wisdom of the region or country the university is planted. There is knowledge among the tribal people, what Francis calls 'popular insight'. The close interplay of scientific research and such knowledge creates abundant riches of wisdom. It is here that the interdisciplinary spirit in the university campus is called for – for such riches from each and every discipline in the school would benefit mankind in no small measure. To this, the following

---

[107] J. H. NEWMAN, *The Idea of a University*, Longman Green and Co., London 1907.

words of Francis to the staff and students of the Pontifical university of Chile are apt:

> The challenge for the community is to not isolate itself from modes of knowledge, or, for that matter, to develop a body of knowledge with minimal concern about those for whom it is intended. It is vital that the acquisition of knowledge lead to an interplay between the university classroom and the wisdom of the peoples who make up this richly blessed land. That wisdom is full of intuitions and perceptions that cannot be overlooked when we think of Chile. An enriching synergy will thus come about between scientific rigour and popular insight; the close interplay of these two parts will prevent a divorce between reason and action, between thinking and feeling, between knowing and living, between profession and service. Knowledge must always sense that it is at the service of life, and must confront it directly in order to keep progressing. Hence, the educational community cannot be reduced to classrooms and libraries but must progress continually towards participation. This dialogue can only take place on the basis of an episteme capable of "thinking in the plural", that is, conscious of the interdisciplinary and interdependent nature of learning. "In this sense, it is essential to show special care for indigenous communities and their cultural traditions. They are not merely one minority among others, but should be the principal dialogue partners, especially when large projects affecting their land are proposed"[108]

---

[108] POPE FRANCIS, Visit to the Pontifical Catholic University of Chile, Address of the Holy Father, Wednesday, 17 January 2018.

Philosophy and mechanics, are the areas of knowledge identifiable. Newman rates the philosophical high. Mechanical education is a great asset – Newman doesn't dispute the fact. He gives attention to it and shows its usefulness to mankind. He only says that this technical knowledge which tends more and more to particular concrete exterior matter, if it is taken too far, would end in no knowledge. It would be knowledge that sought to contribute something – and actually contributed something – but destroyed itself in the attempt. True knowledge is of a scientific and philosophical course. True knowledge is "something intellectual, something which grasps what it perceives through the senses; something which takes a view of things; which sees more than the senses convey; which reasons upon what it sees, and while it sees; which invests it with an idea. It expresses itself, not in a mere enunciation but in an enthymeme; it is of the nature of science from the first, and in this consists its dignity. The principal of real dignity in Knowledge, its worth, its desirableness, considered irrespectively of its results, is this germ within it of a scientific or a philosophical process."[109]

There is something in the Catholic Church that is nowhere. Catholicism rightly understand is a great foster father of the most refined in culture. It alone gives great substance to human flourishing. It holds in the hollow of its hands the satisfactory responses to the complex queries life offers, because its way of life is the only way of life that satisfies life's restiveness. From this boundless store of wisdom, Newman found the proper power of education. In the early pages of *The Idea of a University*, here is what he said in this regard:

> I cannot forget that, at a time when Celt and Saxon were alike savage, it was the See of Peter that gave both of them, first faith, then civilization…I cannot forget how it was from Rome that the glorious St. Patrick was sent to Ireland, and did a work so great that he could not have a successor in it, the sanctity and learning and zeal and charity which followed

---

[109] J. H. NEWMAN, *The Idea of a University*, Longman Green and Co., London 1907.

on his death being but the result of the one impulse which he gave. I cannot forget how, in no long time, under the fostering breath of the Vicar of Christ, a country of heathen superstitions became the very wonder and asylum of all people, - the wonder by reason of its knowledge, sacred and profane, and the asylum of religion, literature and science, when chased away from the continent by the barbarian invaders…Nor can I forget either how my own England had meanwhile become the solicitude of the same unwearied eye: how Augustine was sent to us by Gregory.[110]

Some may think in this connection that I have made the preponderance of education excessive in the story of a genius of signal versatility, to whom education was only one interest among many. No doubt class lectures, rectoral speeches, staff meetings, homework, school research, like manna that fed the Israelites in the wilderness, lose their savor and power of nutriment on the second day. Yet after all it was to his performances as educationist, in - Newman himself had declared education was his line - all the widest significance of that lofty and noble word, that Cardinal Newman owes the lasting substance of his eminence.

It has recently been argued that the 21st century can no longer be seen as gripped in the strait-jacket of household schools of theology. Such labels are seen as doing less than justice to the rich variety of individual talents and intellectual trends which collectively constitute 21st century culture. While not praying for the entombment of the legendary household names of schools of theology, there seems little point in placing an interdict on theological labels which, willy-nilly, have stuck. What is essential is to create today, space for names like John Henry Newman and open wide the doors for more theological inspirations from other lands around the Catholic globe. Pope Francis is already making room for this in his *The Joy of Truth*. In that apostolic

---

[110] J. H. NEWMAN, *The Idea of a University*, Longman Green and Co., London 1907.

constitution he conveys a most crucial message to today's theologian: "The theologian who is satisfied with his complete and conclusive thought is mediocre. The good theologian and philosopher has an open, that is, an incomplete, thought, always open to the maius [greaterness] of God and of the truth, always in development,".[111] Pope Francis is completely Newmanian on this standpoint. Is this not what Newman had warned his own generation on what a true theologian was not?:

> Our theological philosophers are like the old nurses who wrap the unhappy infant in swaddling bands or boards – put a lot of blankets over him – and shut the windows that not a breath of fresh air may come to his skin – as if he were not healthy enough to bear wind and water in due measures. They move in a groove, and will not tolerate any one who does not move in the same.[112]

Newman was mortal and therefore had his own limitations. No book is ever going to live up to the sort of inviolable hallowed billing. The best approach is always to pierce into it with a more prosaic, matter-of-factness. Which is why those who read Newman profoundly can sometimes feel a little deflated by some blemish in the work of such a literary colossus. Perhaps he provided the most beautiful expressions and managerial foundations nourishing the principle of a liberal education. These standings are still workable today. The central point is the tilling of the mind. Newman underlines its central focus on the cultivation of the intellect, its autonomy from moral and religious power and the fact that this knowledge is its own end. Perhaps the crucial difficulty with *The Idea of the University* is its utter anti-utilitarianism.[113] Penning this work at a period when

---

[111] FRANCIS, Apostolic Constitution, *Veritatis Gaudium*.
[112] J. H. NEWMAN, LD, xxiv, 316.
[113] SOPHIA DEBOICK, "Newman suggests a university's 'soul' lies in the mark it leaves on students", in *The Guardian*, 20 October 2010, https://www.theguardian.com/commentisfree/2010/oct/20/john-henry-newman-idea-university-soul.

only a few had the opportunity to go to university, Newman was unable to imagine a situation where higher education would benefit just the elite but a huge mass of society. Some have accused him as "the ultimate ivory tower-dweller"[114] since he has not offered ample ideas on how real concrete life employment of the young and coming generation. Some also say that as a known master of balancing extremes into one beautiful whole tension, Newman has not used that literary skill proficiently in portraying the equilibrium between seeking knowledge for its own sake and availing the students opportunities for marketable skills they are certainly worthy of. Some say he is not explicit about the financial part of university's subsistence which to them is still fundamental. Newman might have had such blemishes but his ideas on university keep moving on. The temptation to disregard him as an authority on university studies today is pointless. Such a view is not only shortsighted on historical merits, it also denies the greatness and lastingness of ideas which must speak to any age. A truth in 1852 is a truth in 2019.

I am well aware that to tie in Pope Francis with Cardinal Newman – a thing I unapologetically do here – is a stroke of temerity. To try to show that Pope Francis' theology of education goes with that of the English theologian, is to push temerity still further. The ashes of controversy, in which Francis is most concerned, are still hot. Yet my thoughtful and penetrating study of Newman, Vatican II and post Vatican II has opened my mind to many interesting things about this holy man vis-à-vis contemporary Christianity. One of such detections is that though he hardly calls the name Newman, Pope Francis' pontificate is that which has had the closest affinity to John Henry Newman. What Francis is doing today to the streets of the world is what Newman's idol patron Philip Neri did to the streets of Rome. Newman venerated and admired the simple Philip Neri. It hasn't surprised me that providence has appointed Pope Francis to canonize Cardinal Newman. They who breathe the same intellectual air (Newman was considered by some detractors as a Jesuit) as

---

[114] SOPHIA DEBOICK, "Newman suggests a university's 'soul' lies in the mark it leaves on students", in The Guardian, 20.10.2010, https://www.theguardian.com/commentisfree/2010/oct/20/john-henry-newman-idea-university-soul.

Newman, they who go through the misunderstandings and suffer similar calumnies he suffered, they who believe with him that "truth can fight its own battle," such must be the best, if not the only true recorders of his life. That is why Pope Francis stands in the most auspicious, the most propitious and the most advantageous position to canonize this great saint and scholar of all times.

www.ingramcontent.com/pod-product-compliance
Ingram Content Group UK Ltd.
Pitfield, Milton Keynes, MK11 3LW, UK
UKHW022223230426
12048UKWH00016BA/1024